LOOKING FOR A KISS

LOOKING FOR A KISS

*A Chronicle of
Downtown Heartbreak
and Healing*

KATE WALTER

Heliotrope Books
New York

Copyright © 2015 Kate Walter

All rights reserved. No part of this book may be reproduced or transmitted in any form or by any means, electronic or mechanical, including photocopying, recording or by an information storage or retrieval system now known or heretoafter invented—except by a reviewer who may quote brief passages in a review to be printed in a magazine or newspaper—without permission in writing from the publisher.

Heliotrope Books LLC
heliotropebooks@gmail.com

Parts of this book appeared in earlier form in *Newsday*, *NY Daily News*, *NYPress*, and *The Villager*.

Cover photograph by Kate Walter
Designed and typeset by Naomi Rosenblatt

Advance Praise for *Looking for a Kiss*

"Until very recently, downtown Manhattan was a world of its own, a place where artists and writers, intellectuals and eccentrics lived freely and precariously. For years, Kate Walter has been that world's Samuel Pepys, recording her life there in brave and revealing detail. In telling us this story of love, loss and ultimate recovery, from its quintessentially downtown title to its crazy yet redemptive final scene, she also reclaims that world with all its quirks and idiosyncrasies."

—John Strausbaugh, author of *The Village: 400 Years of Beats and Bohemians, Radicals and Rogues*

"When gay marriage was still out of reach in New York state, Kate Walter was left behind by her partner of over twenty-five years. Searching for answers to how the connection unraveled and how to connect once more, Walter has written a gift; this fast-paced, funny, touching memoir of triumph over love lost."

—Alice Feiring, author of *The Battle for Wine and Love* and *Naked Wine*

"*Looking For A Kiss* is a smart, funny, sexy and spiritual journey. Walter writes her unique story of lesbian love and heartache in New York's Greenwich Village in a vulnerable, confessional way. Anyone seeking hope can relate to her tale of breakup and renewal."

—Royal Young, author of *Fame Shark*

"In *Looking for a Kiss*, Kate Walter has written the queer low budget E*at Pray Love*. Raw and intimate, she takes you along on her journey to enlightenment. The book is "Dedicated to women who've been dumped after twenty-five years." Yes, the book tells of the demise of her long relationship, but also uncovers a different—and more conscious—way to live. I enjoyed reading about Kate's "New Age" healing process and cheered as she celebrated victories. There's even the bonus of some common-sense dating wisdom by the mysterious "Dr. R.," which I couldn't help but take to heart. A fun and fruitful read."

—Susan Lander, Esq., author of *Conversations with History*

"A real New York story. An unexpected mid-life breakup with her long-term partner sends Kate Walter on a search for recovery, spirituality, and a new love. We root for her as she tries different paths, endures questionable dates, and examines her past for clues to her current situation. As she discovers her higher self along the way, the readers' own imperfections are also illuminated. We relive her moments, told through specific, colorful dialogue and a narrative full of high-def memories. We close the book having come to know this smart, quirky, and very funny woman."

—Kevin Scott Hall, author of *A Quarter Inch from My Heart* and *Off the Charts*

"*Looking for a Kiss* is so engaging that I read it in one sitting. It was addictive. I could not stop. Kate's story is my story, and the story of so many older women who endure a breakup in their 50s and 60s. As a straight woman who went through the breakup of a long marriage at 60, I could relate to everything Kate writes, especially her fixation on her ex and why she left. When someone dumps you without a real explanation, the hurt lingers. Kate really gets what that's about. Her search for both a spiritual center and lasting love—or at least some hot sex—will resonate with every woman who's been through a breakup—gay, straight and in between. Terrific writing."

—Erica Manfred, author *He's History; You're Not; Surviving Divorce After Forty*

"A poignantly told story of one woman's journey from lost love to self-reliance in the heart of New York's downtown, including scenes in the legendary artists complex, Westbeth."

—Gabrielle Selz, author of *Unstill Life: A Daughter's Memoir of Art* and *Love in the Age of Abstraction*

*Dedicated to women who've been dumped
after twenty-five years*

PART ONE

1

RELATIONSHIP AS REALITY SHOW:

SPRING 2005

"So give me demerits for two weeks without sex," defied Slim, my tall, slender, dark-haired lover. We lay together naked in our queen-sized bed, her long legs dangling over the edge. I stared into Slim's brown eyes that still mesmerized me after two decades and asked, "How many demerits? Three? Five?"

"Two," she suggested with a laugh.

"Okay." I felt thrilled she was so agreeable to adjusting the rules of our new "game."

A few weeks before, I'd proposed we start playing a "reality show game" to spark up our twenty-five-year relationship. I'd been feeling neglected, particularly in bed. She even preferred a vibrator, the Magic Wand, a gift she had requested from me a year ago for her fiftieth birthday. For some time now, Slim had been enjoying the Wand with herself. While I felt glad I wasn't the only one of us with sexual desires, she still could not manage much sex with me, always using her busy schedule as a freelance photojournalist as an excuse.

"You always put work first and me second," I'd complained, hurt that we hadn't had sex or a playdate in weeks.

"I want to have fun with you, honey, but then an assignment comes up."

Ironically my essay about how we revived our partnership by getting separate apartments—my queer love story—had just appeared in the Valentine's Day edition of *Newsday*. Our intimacy had improved with this new "living-apart-together" arrangement—we fought less and had more sex. But lately I felt Slim was taking me for granted again.

"We're coasting on the past and the future," I pointed out, referring to our early romantic years and the money she'd saved for our retirement. "We need to do stuff now, before we get old, while we can enjoy ourselves. I want a companion, like the old days."

"Just what are you saying?" she asked. "Do you want to break up?"

I hated her passive-aggression.

When I rode the crosstown bus from my West Village studio to her East Village one-bedroom, I realized I could engage Slim's workaholic drive if I repositioned the relationship as her job. If she didn't live up to her end, she'd be fired. I had an idea that this approach would appeal to her achievement-oriented personality.

We'd always agreed we should make love at least once a week and go to a museum or movie just as often, yet it was difficult to pull off. But what if I assigned points? This way, we'd have something measurable. She'd get five points for sex, five for an art date, three for dinner in a restaurant. If she wanted to be with me, she'd have to earn it. I was psyched to run this past her as soon as I'd settled into the couch at her place, which used to be our place. I greeted our cat, Tyler, of whom she had primary custody.

"Reality show? What a great idea," said Slim, a television junkie. "I love it. When do we start?"

After finishing dinner, we returned to the sofa and devised the plan. We'd begin that Saturday night and the game would run for fourteen weeks. She had to score 100 points. That was generous because if we had sex and a date once a week, she would rack up 140 points by our deadline. I was cutting her too much slack.

"It should be 120 points," I suggested, explaining that if she were to meet only the minimum requirements she would score more than 100.

"No, I agreed to 100."

"Okay. It's a deal." We shook hands.

"What happens if I don't have 100 points?" Slim asked, suddenly worried.

"Uh, in that case," I improvised, "You get to plead your case as to why you should remain in the relationship."

"Oooh, that's cool. Just like *The Road to Stardom* where the singers get to plead with Missy Elliot as to why they should be allowed to stay on the tour bus."

She was really getting into this. Just like the way she loved *American Idol*, *The Apprentice*, and all those stupid reality programs she tried to get me to watch.

"It's possible you will get a two-week extension," I said. "With a special task to perform. But let's hope we don't have to go there."

"You'll keep score," she said, unbuttoning her blouse. "Now…I want to earn some points."

I leaned over to kiss her and said, "Let's play."

Twenty-five years had gone by fast, and this silver anniversary seemed like a crossroads: Would we make it for another twenty-five years? My vote was to try. Slim had convinced me that no one else would put up with my quirky habits. The idea of dating again—in middle age—loomed as a draining, time-consuming chore that might lead nowhere. So I wanted to fix our relationship and make us better again. The sweet Slim I fell in love with was still there, beneath the workaholic. I saw glimpses of this warm and charming woman and wanted to make her resurface.

Over the decades, my thrice-divorced college friend, Rosina, chided me that if I bent over backwards any more for Slim, my spine would break. Rosina thought I was a masochist.

What I knew was that I was the cute, chatty, Catholic girl from New Jersey knocked out by a tall, beautiful, black-haired, brown-eyed, Jewish girl from Brooklyn. Slim said I was hot-looking when we first saw each other in Chelsea at a meeting of the Gay Teachers Association. But I regarded her as the real beauty. Slim was the oldest of three, the classic star child who could do no wrong in her secular family. I was the middle of three, the maverick in a religious household. Right from our first date, I knew that Slim was the one—my mental and emotional soul mate.

She made me feel centered and secure. I was an anxious person and her presence calmed me down. I had my best friend and lover in one package. I just needed more attention, to feel that she wanted me as much as I wanted her. At our twenty-five-year mark, she was distracted by her career, which had been successful for many years, but I knew she still loved me. Just recently, we were driving on the West Side Highway and she pulled over for a speeding ambulance and declared, "I'd be devastated if anything happened to you."

LOOKING FOR A KISS

I taught remedial English at a community college Tuesday and Friday afternoons. Slim had a steady gig at a tabloid on Saturday, Sunday, and Monday. So that left midweek for dates. That was fine; places were less crowded. But during week one of our game her car stalled out, and Slim cancelled our plans.

Week two started the next Saturday, but we didn't have sex because she had her period. Still, we were determined to have a midweek lunch and museum date, so we went to the Met and saw the Diane Arbus show. We had seen many of the photos before, but we were pulled to the well-known "Identical Twins." Those little girls in matching black dresses and white hair bands were now middle-aged women, like us. Slim had an upcoming assignment to shoot the sisters for a story about the exhibit.

When I came over Friday evening, she hugged me and declared how she couldn't wait to have sex that weekend. But she was too tired now, so I looked forward to the following night. The next morning, Slim woke up with a sinus headache, took two aspirins, and went to work. I felt lonely walking back to my place, sensing that we would not be intimate that weekend.

That night when I returned to her apartment, I detected the tantalizing aroma of vegetables sizzling in the kitchen. "I'm making seitan stroganoff," Slim announced, slamming a pan onto the kitchen table, "and I want to get extra points because I'm sick." (We had accorded meal preparation three points.)

Slim was a creative vegetarian chef, while I thought cooking was boring. The dinner was delicious, especially the creamy mushroom sauce. Slim wasn't hungry, but we sat at the table together in our cozy kitchen. When I complimented her culinary skills, she asked again for bonus points for making supper with a sinus headache. I countered that she deserved demerits for not satisfying me two weeks in a row, an issue we had not discussed up front.

"You know I care more about sex than food," I said, but she thought food was love. Her mother in Long Island was an overfeeder, who made always made too many dishes for a holiday meal. So I conceded an extra point for dinner. Slim offered love through gourmet cooking, although I'd rather feast upon her gourmet body.

End of week two: Slim had scored 21 points total. She was doing well. So why weren't we getting it on more? Maybe the game rules were too easy or the time frame too long. I'd never played a reality game before. At the end of two weeks, I was in a bad mood. Slim said, "This is what I don't like about you. I was sick this weekend."

"So why don't you offer to reschedule for early next week?" I suggested.

"Because I'm sooo busy with work, " she said.

"Well, this is what I don't like about you," I replied.

The next week she gave me daily updates, like how Daniel Day Lewis was obnoxious and refused to pose for anyone during a shoot. She didn't score at all by midweek; she was so busy with work that we did not even see each other until the weekend. On Saturday night, I could tell Slim didn't want to make love because she had a cold, but she insisted, "I'll do this because I don't want to hear you complaining, and …"

"And because you need to rack up some points this week."

As we savored the afterglow, Slim told me how much she'd enjoyed herself and how she was glad I had pushed her. That was when we revisited my idea of sex demerits if we went two weeks without intimacy.

"And I think we should reconsider the time span of the game. It's way too long."

"No, you have to give me enough time to score points," she argued.

At the end of week three she had twenty-nine points total, but she still needed seventy-one more. Without question, she was paying more attention to me. Then again, I had deliberately given her a lot of time so she couldn't possibly lose.

We were planning to go to a photo exhibit on Pier 54 in Hudson River Park when Slim next came over to my place. She was wearing a vintage tan jacket from the '40s and a jaunty newsboy cap. My partner had style; she loved shopping at flea markets and mixing and matching different eras from her extensive wardrobe. "You look so cute," I said, kissing her hello.

Just as we were leaving, her beeper went off: An assignment must be done that afternoon, and was she available? Slim ditched me and rushed home for her cameras. But we recouped the next day and walked along the river to the show.

Out in the world she was this street-smart kid from Brooklyn, tuned into the nuances on the sidewalks, looking for a funny photo. Slim idolized photographers Wee-Gee and his mentor, Lisette Model. I walked around spacy and reflective, a writer from gritty Paterson, New Jersey, inspired by hometown star Allen Ginsberg, whose poetry readings I'd attended at the local public library. It was always fun to walk in the city with my lover and best friend, even if we walked in such different ways.

Saturday night, we smoked this great pot—New York Diesel—a gift from a friend in the East Village. We listened to jazz—Pharoah Sanders and John Coltrane—wailing on the sax and then threw in Alice Coltrane's CD as we moved from the couch into the bedroom.

Our romp in the sack was really good. I could tell she was exceptionally turned on, which made me only more excited. After we finished, she suggested an extra point. I wondered how this compared to what Slim called "the best sexual experience" of her life.

That "best" had happened a few months earlier. I'd been lying on my stomach, the soles of my feet flat up against the dresser, my legs stretching two feet from the bed. The rest of my body was on the mattress, and my head was between Slim's legs. I kept pushing off from the dresser to add more pressure to my movements. I could only get so much, so I decided to play her clit like a violin. I kept going up and down, side to side with my tongue. I could tell from her bucking that she was into this and as she started to come, I felt like my tongue movements were totally in synch with her muscle contractions.

"Yes, yes, yes," she cried, pounding her hand on the bed.

When I stopped she said, "That was great. The best ever. Whatever you were doing was fantastic. Come here."

She pulled me up next to her and I put my head on her breasts.

"It was fun for me too," I said.

By the end of week four, Slim had forty points. At this rate, she would win easily—but then what? I was afraid she'd slip back once the game ended. I wanted her like this without score-keeping. Of course, I needed her to win because I wanted to stay together, yet a demented part of me wanted her to lose to verify my complaint.

Another week passed with no midweek rendezvous. She was busy shooting ten restaurants in two days, a museum show, and a movie star turned author, Jane Fonda. Slim was working intensely with her web designer, going back and forth on the photos. She called me one night, almost in tears. She was overwhelmed with work and now her computer was acting funny. I was supposed to be empathetic, but I thought our relationship should come before work.

When I got to her place, she was at the computer editing photos and barely looked up. The good vibes from the hot sex had faded. Hew new website was live. It looked fantastic. That's when Slim told me she had been so horny all week and couldn't wait to have sex with me tomorrow. I was pleased and fantasized about our upcoming night of pleasure.

Saturday night she was in the tub. Slim always took a bath before we made love. I was looking through our stacks of CDs for something funky when she emerged from the bathroom in her robe and announced she was too tired. What? Was she serious?

"I'm exhausted from too many twelve-hour days," Slim said, "and from waking up too early. If I do anything tonight except watch TV, I'll get sick."

"This is news to me. So when did you figure this out?"

"Just now when I was relaxing in the hot water."

"Thanks, fuck you."

I retreated into the bathroom with a copy of *Time* magazine and the Jane Fonda book excerpt. Slim had taken Fonda's picture that week and a zillion other shots. I had been asking Slim for over a year to shoot a new photo of me. The picture I had been using when editors requested one was ten years old.

"When are you gonna take a new head shot of me?" I yelled from the bathroom. "You take everyone else. Do I have to be famous to get you to do my picture?"

Slim opened the bathroom door and explained that when she had the rare day off, the last thing she wanted to do was shoot pictures.

"When things slow down, I'll do it," she said.

Slim took off from work on Sunday to attend the baptism of my great niece. After the church service, we were stuck inside a New Jersey catering hall on the first real spring day. We agreed this sacrifice merited three points. While driving back to the city, Slim and I planned a playdate for Wednesday. But that morning she woke up at five and cancelled. Her chronic sleeping disorder was now exacerbated by perimenopause.

We didn't meet midweek, but Slim made up for it Saturday night. She cooked pasta with sautéed vegetables—and we had a great time making love.

"Isn't it something how I'm enjoying this so much?" Slim said as we were resting in bed. "Do you think it's related to menopause? Like my hormones are going crazy?"

"Yeah, it's pretty funny that after all these years, you're suddenly into it."

"I'm having my teenage years in reverse," Slim said. "Isn't it amazing that it took twenty-five years to get to this place?"

"Some women never get there, " I said. "You're fabulous at fifty-one."

Unlike me, Slim was sexually shy when we met. Now she was like a randy adolescent, albeit one with a high-powered career.

With the contest not yet half over, Slim was in good shape with fifty-three points. I didn't want her to lose, but I wanted her to sweat it out. How did it get to the point that we turned our relationship into a reality show? Then again, how many long-term lesbian couples were having sex—of any kind—after twenty-five years?

"I feel like I'm just now starting to have great orgasms," Slim observed as we lay in bed together.

"Geez, I should have gotten you that Magic Wand sooner," I said. Since I had never bought a vibrator before, I went with a classic for Slim. The Magic Wand is a long plastic thing with a huge whirring head and two speeds. It plugs into an electrical outlet, like a household appliance meant for the G-spot. I think it was originally invented for body massage.

Slim was making up for lost time, having afternoon playdates with herself and the Wand. She even enhanced her vibrator experience by devouring lesbian erotica. She reminded me that I always wanted her to read more. I was glad she was having fun, but I actually became jealous of her connection with this buzzing metal. I couldn't compete, so this made me nervous, even though she was finally at a point where she wanted sex more often. She even admitted her dependence on the toy was addictive—to the point where she scheduled stuff around her private sessions. One night she described her incredible orgasms with the vibrator.

"I feel like you're comparing our lovemaking to the toy, and that's not fair," I said. "I'm not a machine."

"I'm not comparing, but can't you see how I'd be psyched about this? Nothing like it has ever happened to me before."

"Wait a minute," I stopped her. "Are you saying you never had an orgasm with me in all these years? I wouldn't expect it to be as intense as the toy but . . ."

"No, I never did," she said, "but it was me. Not you."

"What? What about that time a few months ago? The one you said was the best ever—"

"Well, maybe I did then, on some level," she said—a typical hazy response.

"What about that time upstate when we made love to that Julia Fordham album and we both felt like we were in synch with the music?"

She shook her head. "Not really."

Hot tears rolled from my eyes onto the pillow. I felt like a failure as a lover, and I was shocked and hurt that she had never discussed this in a relationship we both described as "honest."

"How come you never told me this? It seemed like you were getting off, and then you'd say you had a good time."

"I did have a good time. I liked what you were doing but…"

"No wonder you were never that into sex all those years. If you had brought this up before, we could have worked on it. Instead, we fought about not having enough sex."

"I guess I wasn't ready to deal with it myself."

"What other secrets do you have? And where does this leave us now?" I asked, thinking this distressing news bent the reality game stakes into the ground.

"Well, since I have gotten so far with the toy, I think I could get to that point with you. I never would have gotten to this stage without you being a sensitive lover. There are no other secrets, and it really wasn't a secret. I didn't even know what I was missing."

"But you knew something was not happening and you never told me—that was not fair." I felt like an idiot to have been so presumptuous.

Now she'd thrown off the power balance in our partnership. She was already the money-making photographer, but at least I could give her what she wanted in bed. Or so I had thought.

"Your ego is wounded," she said. "You like to see yourself as a Don Juan. But it wasn't your fault at all."

It did not matter whether it was her or me. Yes, I knew she did not have cosmic orgasms like I did, but I thought she came…sometimes.

"I worked hard to preserve a relationship that was rooted in a falsehood," I replied.

"Don't be so dramatic," Slim said. "I'm sorry. I couldn't talk about it until now. You know, honey, I love making love to you."

But while I needed her to make me come, I could see that she needed the vibrator.

"Maybe you won't even want me to go down on you now," I said, frustrated.

"That's ridiculous. Why dwell on the past?" she continued. "You always do that, Kate. Why not be happy that now I'm into sex? And you made all this possible. I was thinking we could bring the toy into bed with us."

Enter the Magic Wand at half-time in our reality show game.

"What?" I gasped. "To me, that thing is as erotic as a blow dryer."

"You're too rigid, Kate. I always did what you wanted all these years. Now I'm asking you to do what I want."

"Feels like in five minutes you went from being an ice queen to a sex addict," I said. Then I conceded, "Fine. I'll do whatever you want, but you must take a new picture of me." I kissed her good night.

"Okay, okay, I'll take your picture, " said Slim. "I promise."

Her new take-charge sexual attitude floored me. I needed to extract something in exchange if I was giving up my last bastion of control. Suddenly, everything was upside down. She was the sexually demanding one and I was the one who could not sleep. I tossed until 4 A.M., replaying my life, trying to understand how things had gotten to this point.

2

THE PHOTO SHOOT AND BAD NEWS:

SPRING 2006

"Wet your lips," Slim ordered and I did. My partner was finally taking my new author photo, which I'd been asking her to do for five years. For too long, I'd been using an old black and white she'd taken in the early '90s in front of our East Village tenement on St. Marks Place, where we had lived for two decades. Since Slim was a busy photojournalist, we joked that our situation was like the cobbler's kids who'd outgrown their shoes.

"Look this way," she said, pointing north. "Smile. Very nice. Good, just a few more," she said as she snapped away. Slim had me posed me against the white brick walls in the courtyard of my building. She paused, walked toward me, ran her fingers through my hair, fluffed it up, and then she stepped back to shoot.

"Are we done here yet?" I asked, my mouth tired from smiling.

"Let's go the pier," Slim said, as we wrapped up the shoot in the courtyard. "The light should be interesting now."

As we left the area, I noticed a married couple practicing tai chi and an older woman at her easel painting flowers. I lived in Westbeth Artists Housing, where it was common to see painters and actors practicing their craft outdoors. In the late '90s, I'd landed a tiny studio in this renowned West Village institution, which became my official residence.

We divided our time between the two apartments but kept our romantic life in our original dwelling because it had a real bed, a queen-sized captain's bed whose drawers contained Slim's negatives, beneath our mattress. "Bivillage" was the best of both worlds, and we discovered that having separate spaces was good for our relationship. We missed each other.

Slim adjusted the camera bag over her shoulder as we exited the grounds, walked to West Street, crossed the highway, and entered Hudson River Park. We strolled onto the Christopher Street pier past the gay/lesbian/trans teenagers who hung out at the east end, a mecca for queer teens from the five boroughs and New Jersey. Two black men were voguing to dance music, trying to outdo each other, while their friends cheered them on. Two pretty Latina women were embracing.

When we found a quiet spot toward the other end, Slim put her bag down near her feet, scanned the scene, and took out the tools of her trade. She posed me in the center of the pier with the wooden decks and steel railings as set props. She held her camera in her right hand and the flash in her left hand above her head; the flash was plugged into the battery pack on her belt. She moved gracefully with the equipment, steady and balanced, clearly in command of her craft.

I loved watching Slim in action with her cameras. I was proud of her, recalling how she transitioned from a public school teacher to an award-winning news photographer. I regarded her journalism career as the child we never had. I'd planted the seed over twenty years ago when I asked her to take pictures to accompany my music reviews. While I had no regrets about being child free, I loved that our relationship had given birth to something unexpected and wonderful.

"Over here. I want your eyes over here," she pointed, directing me professionally.

"How does my hair look?" I asked. "It's so windy."

"It's fine, very natural," she said. "This is an environmental shot."

"Feel like I'm squinting into the sun," I said, as Slim sprinted around me for different angles. Slim was tall and thin, athletic, a gym and dance fanatic in great shape for a fifty-two-year-old woman. She had physical traits suitable to her field. As the shoot continued, a few gay kids became curious and sashayed over to watch, but they got bored as soon as they realized I was not a celebrity.

"You look good," she said. "The lighting is exquisite."

Slim's face was obscured by the camera, but the energy she gave off was intense as she totally focused on the task. One kid made a stupid comment but she tuned him out as she kept directing me. I wondered what I looked like through her eyes.

The next night, I went to Slim's apartment to choose the picture for my website.

We were sitting in the bedroom, her on the computer, me on the bed next to her, leaning over her shoulder.

"I like that one," I said, as we browsed through the shots.

"Good choice, honey," Slim said, then enlarged it.

The photo shows me—a fifty-seven-year-old dyke—on the pier with the Hudson River to the side and Manhattan in the background. The late afternoon lighting recalls Edward Hopper (who painted in the Village). I have a great smile and the wind is blowing through my wavy brown hair, sweeping it back. I'm wearing my favorite vintage black Halston jacket, a gift from Slim.

"You look really good there," she said.

"Just fix up that tooth, make it whiter," I told her.

"Want me to take out any lines?" Slim cracked.

"No, that's the way I look. I like the laugh lines around my eyes."

"Just asking," she said. "I can do anything you want in Photoshop."

"I want to look like me. I'm a writer, not an actress."

Slim tweaked the picture and we selected another portrait, a head shot of me in the courtyard against the white brick background. After she finished the photo editing, we relaxed and talked on the couch. Then she went into the kitchen, made us hot chocolate, and brought out two steaming mugs. We snuggled together as we sipped the cocoa.

"Thanks for doing this," I said, wondering why it had taken her so long to shoot my photo. It turned out that it was her final gift to me after twenty-six years together.

Slim hadn't called me in the past two days and barely answered my emails. I was getting anxious. I was camped out on the couch of my studio when the phone finally rang. Her voice sounded weird as she blurted out, "I want to break up with you. I want to be free to see other people."

What? Something had felt wrong for a while, but I never expected this blow. I started trembling as her words sank in.

"How could you do this to me?" I managed to reply.

"I don't want to have any regrets in life," she said as I lay on the couch, sobbing hysterically at the thought of losing her, especially when I'd thought we were on the verge of a breakthrough. We'd come a long way from when I was jealous of her plastic playmate. In fact, we were trying to incorporate the sex toy into our lovemaking and seemed to be growing closer.

Instead, it felt like that vibrator had wrecked our relationship, rather than enhanced it—as difficult as that is to believe. A stupid, buzzing piece of metal apparently had been the tipping point of Slim's decision. She thought she'd have a better chance of having a cosmic orgasm—like those she had alone with the vibrator—with someone new, fresh, exciting. I was so hurt.

Then came the crushing phone call.

"But what about that great time we had a few weeks ago?" I said, reminding her of a passionate night of lovemaking when Slim said she had had a fantastic orgasm from oral sex.

"That's not the same thing," she said, dismissing my ability to please her. While I could not compete with the repetitive force of a machine, I was a good kisser.

Slim also told me she was bored with the relationship but didn't know why. Everything I did bothered her, like if I didn't turn off the kettle the second it started to whistle, or if I spilled crumbs on the floor when I ate. She said there was no one else. She just wanted to be free. She claimed she was still attracted to me but she wanted to feel excited, and we were not that exciting anymore.

"What do you think you're missing?" I asked.

"Probably nothing. It's a fantasy," she admitted.

I was stunned that after twenty-six years I was being cast aside for a flight of fancy. I was still in love with Slim, and our rich history gave us depth. Vacation pictures on our bulletin board—crammed with snapshots and political buttons—offered a capsule summary of our relationship. We shared romantic vacations to Key West and the Caribbean; sunbathed on a gay beach in Spain; went to Amsterdam and London on what we considered our honeymoon.

We weekended in upstate New York or the Jersey Shore. We camped it up at gay marches. We posed with relatives at my parents' fiftieth anniversary.

I liked the silly rituals we had developed over the years, like adding another rainbow sticker to the window on our anniversary. I liked the household roles we had carved out. Slim cooked gourmet vegetarian dinners. I fixed little things that broke. I always melted whenever she touched my knee as we rode in her car and she said, "I love you so much."

We exchanged special gifts on Christmas Eve and our January birthdays. (We were both Capricorns.) We nurtured our creative gifts and critiqued each other's work. We survived sadistic bosses, horrible upstairs neighbors, and the loss of Bedford and Grove, our lovable cats. We supported each other through family crises, like my father's death and the demise of our closest male friends to AIDS (my former boyfriend and her ex-husband). We attended funerals and weddings, dancing the hora at her brother's nuptials and the Irish jig on my niece's big day

"Why don't we try to work on things?" I pleaded. "How many people still have chemistry—like we do—after so many years together?"

"I have to do this," she insisted, reverting back to her childhood single-girl-in-the-city fantasy but with the added spice of sex. "Now I have to get off the phone."

After we hung up, I sent Slim a zillion emails asking her to reconsider. Then I called Rosina, my oldest friend, and also left a message for my shrink. My theory was that Slim was frightened of intimacy and pushing me away. Slim had always been more sexually inhibited than I, but the vibrator had put her in touch with new sensations. I initially thought this development was great and would enable us to take our relationship to a higher level. But then I sensed that Slim was scared to go there with me and deepen our bond. Now I felt bamboozled. I couldn't wait to talk to Dr. R., my therapist.

My relationship with Slim was the center of my life. She was my best friend and my family, my home. Everything revolved around her. I reread the twenty-fifth anniversary card Slim sent me the previous year. "There is no replacement for you, Kate. I want us to continue as a couple, having hot sex and taking care of each other."

How could things could have changed so much in a year? When had she become so unhappy and conflicted that she wanted more? Slim had married her high school sweetheart at twenty, and we hooked up not long after that ended. I was five years older and had been more experienced when we met. Suddenly, it seemed, she felt curious and struck by her mortality, as if she needed to do in middle age what I'd done in my younger days.

In the weeks after Slim dropped the breakup bomb, we existed in limbo, still seeing each other socially, but not having sex. We fell into this weird pattern of not being able to let go: Slim had made this big announcement but did not know how to execute it; I kept waging a campaign to get her to reconsider. I was so distraught that I sought advice from Lexa, a psychic witch in the East Village, who I usually saw once a year for an annual forecast.

"Make a clean break," Lexa said as she looked at the tarot card layout. "You need to end it completely, so you might be able to restore it. A separation is your position of strength. Withdraw in a caring and loving way and stick to this plan. If you have no contact for some time, she will miss you. You need to make a major change and free up something that has been lingering and not dealt with. The love is still there for both of you."

Sitting across from her was different than talking to my therapist, yet their comments were strikingly similar. Dr. R. often made mystical leaps and Lexa's interpretations had a psychoanalytic bent. Although the psychic first made this suggestion, my shrink also advocated a clear-cut separation when Slim steadfastly refused to go to therapy.

"She's in a state of confusion," said Dr. R. "This isn't fair to you. You can't be living in this state of anxiety. She's hurting you, so why have contact? She has problems with intimacy," my therapist continued. "She cuts off her feelings and her needs to be close."

Both my therapist and my psychic thought Slim might come to her senses if I cut off the friendship. I thought so too. So I decided to bring up the idea of a real separation. As much as I valued Slim's companionship, I could not continue in this painful state of not sleeping together but still meeting for dinner.

When I proposed this, we were sitting on the couch at the East Village apartment, where we'd had so many good times. Slim's eyes filled with tears.

"If it gets too much, we can call each other, right?" she asked.

"No, we can't do that," I said, "unless it's an emergency."

"But we're best friends," she insisted.

"I know," I said, feeling really sad.

We agreed to no contact for a month, and then we'd check back in and talk.

Slim came over to my apartment to hang out on the day before the separation officially began. She brought a copy of a picture of us together, taken two months earlier at a fashion show of vintage clothing at St. Mark's Church. The event was sponsored by specific stores in the East Village. Slim had been a model wearing a campy golf outfit put together from her thrift-store shopping. I have my arm draped over her shoulder. We're smiling and look happy.

She helped me pick out some pieces of writing to put up on my new website, and I showed her some copy I'd created for her site. We were tying up loose ends. Then we left my studio and walked arm-in-arm in Hudson River Park. I loved touching her.

"Why are you doing this?" I asked again. "Won't you at least go to one counseling session with me or by yourself? Talk to someone. Make sure this is the right decision."

"Look, Skeets," she said, calling me by an old nickname she had not used in years. "I know we're good together, but I need to be out in the world to explore what's out there. I realize I've been driving you crazy with my new sexual demands and we can't go on like this."

"But we can work this out, " I pleaded.

"You'll meet someone else," she said to my surprise.

"I don't want someone else. I want you," I said.

As the afternoon ended, we left the park and I escorted her to her car. We hugged and kissed goodbye and we both said "I love you." Slim started to tear up and dashed into her car. I started crying as I stood on the corner in front of my building and watched her drive away. We waved, she blew me a kiss, and I did the same.

I knew I would miss Slim and be lonely, but what was the alternative? Everyone seemed to think the separation would give me power. Slim had always held the power in our relationship. Although my shrink had endorsed this clean break, she warned me, "You played this card and it might not work out the way you wanted."

My friend Rosina told me to relax and pretend Slim was on vacation. Sara said it was good that I was setting limits and not being a self-destructive martyr. My shrink thought Slim was treating me horribly, but maybe she'd be able to figure this out if she spent some time alone. I recall what she said: "She has to feel the loss."

I felt scared of losing her. One Saturday night, I sat at my computer, thinking that my future was hanging in the balance. I started shaking all over, which frightened me. I went to a chair, sat down with my spine straight, and started my yogic breathing exercises.

Another night, I had a vivid dream. I was lying in bed trying to fall asleep and suddenly it felt like Slim was hugging me. We were on the couch at her apartment and she had just come from the bathtub in her robe and we were about to make love. I was in a twilight state. I knew I was dreaming, but I willed this hug to continue a bit longer because it felt so comforting. When I woke up, I felt so bereft without her. I wanted Slim in my arms.

But I pushed myself to do things. I went to literary readings and threw myself back into yoga classes, which helped with anxiety. Weekends were the worst.

I talked to Dr. R. regularly and consulted Lexa, the psychic, a week before the month's separation ended. Once again, they were shockingly in agreement. "Slim doesn't have much of a life beyond work and thinks it is connected to being with you," opined Dr. R.

"I'm not stopping her from doing things on her own," I said. "She's a workaholic."

"She resents you," said Lexa. "She views having her own life as cheating. You managed to have a world independent of her. Slim feels she is making tremendous sacrifices to be in the relationship and you're not, so this creates envy."

"It is great you are doing this and staying strong," said Dr. R. "It's not good for her to see you are willing to do anything to stay together. It's hard to imagine a whole month could go by and she wouldn't miss you."

"Slim misses you," said Lexa, "and thinks maybe she made a mistake. She fears that if you break up, you will find another lover but she won't. Rather than dealing with her uncomfortable feelings, Slim is caught up in this place where her heart gets hard. She is unhappy but can't get out. She is enslaved to a negative way of thinking—the devil card keeps coming up.

"The relationship is jammed up with anger and resentment," Lexa continued. "But she doesn't know how to fight to save it. She doesn't want to attack you but doesn't know how else to express her anger in a constructive way."

While I knew I was paying this chorus of advisors to be on my side, the uncanny similarity of their interpretations gave me hope.

The month dragged as I ran dialogues in my head practicing what I'd say when we spoke again. Should I tell her how much I suffered this month? Or should I be more cool? The last night of the separation I sent an email as soon as the clock went past midnight. Right after I hit the send button I thought my message sounded too eager.

Hi Slim, Welcome back. I really missed you. I hope your heart and mind are open after this hard month of separation and you have gained insights. Let's talk. What was this month like for you? I lost weight. Pants that were too tight fit me now. Love, Kate.

The next morning I woke up to find her reply. I was trembling as I hit the read button:

Hi Kate,

The thought of talking about this is making me sick. I went to the dermatologist yesterday and have shingles. It's a virus and it was brought on from stress. My month seemed to fly except for the last weekend. My feelings about us haven't changed. I don't know what else you want me to say or do at this point. I love you but I need to be true to myself. Being in a relationship is not what I need now. I've been in a relationship my whole entire adult life! I hope that you were okay. I need to go swimming now.

What! She didn't even sign it? I started to cry and wrote back a few emails begging her to call me. At this point, I was desperate and no longer cared how I came across. Slim said she felt bombarded so I stopped. She kept citing the shingles as an excuse not to talk on the phone. I thought that was cold. I called Dr. R. to schedule an emergency session.

"I'm so sorry," she said. "This isn't what I thought would happen. I'll get my date book."

I walked around the Village and almost got hit by a cab as I approached my building and crossed Washington Street without looking. I was dazed. A loud honk broke into my furious thoughts as I jumped back onto the curb automatically. Maybe I should have let myself get hit to make Slim feel guilty.

Why did Slim get colder since the separation? This plan had backfired. Her wanting to be out in the world to meet other people had switched to her wanting to be alone. She seemed very mixed up. Either way, she was casting me aside.

Slim asked for some breathing space to get better from the shingles, so I wished her good health and backed off. She replied, "Thanks, honey." I took the term of endearment as a good sign and waited for her call. A week passed. No word.

Dr. R. had originally been in the "sit tight" camp, but when she heard I almost got hit by a cab, she changed her mind. My therapist thought it was risky to call but not good to squash my anger. So I drafted an email and let two friends edit it. As we went back and forth with word choices, I felt like I was in a writing workshop. But the stakes were so high my prose had to convey the right message with the right tone. What I sent was calm, not provocative, but I told Slim I felt it was wrong for her not to speak to me after the separation. She had violated our agreement.

She wrote, "We'll talk. Please take it easy and relax. I know it's hard. Hugs, Slim."

Relax? Was she kidding? I did feel calmer after that email but then the phone rang that afternoon. I was nervous but hopeful when I saw her name come up on my caller ID.

"So how have you been?" I asked, trying to keep things light. "How was your month?"

"I don't want to report to you," Slim snarled back.

"Why are you talking to me like that?" I asked, trying to remain calm. "I'm your best friend."

"I'm angry at my family, my parents, and angry feelings come out when I'm talking to you because you were my family," she said, indeed sounding angry and irrational.

"Why should our relationship be poisoned by them? Why give your parents so much power?" I asked, but got no reply.

When I first met her parents, they shocked me. I'd had never met a married couple so openly contemptuous of each other. It scared me to be around them when they tossed barbs. I felt like the guest in a Jewish version of *Who's Afraid of Virginia Woolf*, although these characters were not as witty. I could see why Slim shut down emotionally as child, a survival mechanism that she adapted as she witnessed her father berate her mother.

Every Thanksgiving, as we returned from dinner there, we rode back on the Long Island Expressway marveling that this disturbed duo had stayed together. I blamed our arguing on my in-laws and their horrible example. My parents respected each other, rarely raised their voices, and had enjoyed being together. They were still in love when my father died.

Slim had told her parents about the breakup, and their only reaction was that they thought she would go straight! I was hurt that my mother-in-law of twenty-six years didn't even ask how I was doing. All those times I had sat at her dinner table, I always thought she liked me. Or was that just some phony warmth?

"I haven't told my family yet," I said. "I was waiting to hear from you. I don't get this. You sound like a different person. We parted on loving terms."

"I was so upset about the thought of talking to you as the month came to an end, she answered. "The idea of having contact was too painful."

"Well, I thought about this a lot this month," I said. "Losing your friendship would be the worst part. I missed talking to you."

"Let me think about this. Everything is too new," she replied. "Listen, I gotta go on an assignment, so I can't hang on the phone."

"Wait—I need to get my clothes from the dresser drawers. Can I come over now?"

"Your clothes are in plastic bags in the apartment hallway. If you come over, I just want you to stay in the entranceway and not go into the living room and—"

I was taken aback. My stuff was already packed up. Slim sure wasn't wasting any time.

"On second thought," she added. "I don't want you in the apartment at all. I'll drop the bags in your lobby on my way to work."

"Why are you acting like this?" I asked. I'd lived in that East Village apartment for two decades and never expected to be banished. I felt like she was putting up a moat. Slim did have a mean streak (which I had foolishly dismissed over the years), but this was too much.

I hung up the phone and started beating myself up for investing so much of my adult life with someone who could break up a long-term relationship in such an uncivilized manner.

As word spread, my girlfriends (gay and straight) rallied around with support. To them, I was the loyal fifty-seven=year-old wife whose spouse got bored and walked out. Their reactions went from Rosina's outrage to Jessica's empathy: "She is acting out of extreme emotional distress. Why else would she break all contact?"

"You probably don't want to hear this now," wrote Nina, "but this could be a good thing, giving you the opportunity to meet someone more open. By the way, you are much cuter than Slim. You know that, don't you?"

Both my shrink and my psychic wondered why I had dismissed her mean side and been masochistic when I was with her. Dr. R. never really liked Slim; she thought my partner lacked generosity and our relationship was unbalanced, too one-sided. So I had avoided discussing Slim in my sessions until this crisis. Instead, I'd spent years dissecting my ultra-Catholic childhood and my fear of success.

Now I wondered why my two main advisors had seemed certain the separation would bring her back. Were they just gambling with that concept to ease my pain? Or had I been so desperate I would have grabbed at any advice?

"You just bent and ignored," said Lexa in a post-breakup reading. "You're in shock because you gave everything to this woman and figured she would never leave."

"I can't believe she is acting so hostile," I said.

"It's the shock of being a loyal subject sent to the guillotine," Lexa expounded.

"Banished by the Queen," I said.

"The Queen has killed you off," said Lexa. "But you must have known she had that capability to be bitchy. How could you not know?"

"I guess I focused on her good qualities," I said defensively.

I knew Slim had been going through a midlife crisis, but I did not see the depth of her discontent because I had friends and projects. I recalled something Slim snapped at me in our last phone conversation: "You'd have to be blind not to see this was brewing for years."

I was devastated. After devoting most of my life to our relationship, all I had was a worthless domestic partnership agreement, two boxes full of photos of us together, and bundles of cards saying how much she loved me and wanted to grow old with me.

I felt abandoned. Losing my best friend and support system after two and a half decades felt unbearable and I didn't even have Slim to help me through.

3

COMING HOME AGAIN:

SUMMER/FALL 2006

After being dumped by Slim, I escaped to the Jersey Shore to my family's summer house in Ocean Beach. I went to see my feisty eighty-four-year-old Irish Catholic mother and spill the bad news. We had had a stormy relationship for years but now I needed her help.

I was the outsider middle child who always had the rockiest relationship with my parents. My older sister was the star child, scholarship winner, and best friends with my mother; they dressed alike and read the same authors. My younger brother was the baby and only boy, "the Little Prince" who could do no wrong. Now my siblings lived in suburban New Jersey; both taught in the same urban school system that my father retired from.

My sister gave Sunday school lessons and crocheted hats for cancer patients. My brother had a side business painting houses. They were both married with children.

I was gay, a writer who lived in Manhattan, and I had not held a full-time job in years. I was angry at the Catholic Church, which upset my ultra-religious parents. All this made for conflict over the decades. I went from being a hippie to being queer. For years, I clashed with my mother because she was very controlling. When I was growing up she ran the dinner table conversation like she was a talk show host, asking each of us what had happened in school that day. I often ran over my allotted amount of time, and she'd cut me off. My father let her run the show at home. He always defended her while my brother and sister thought she was supermom and I was the one with issues. I thought they had never really separated and I was more independent.

LOOKING FOR A KISS

That summer, I could not take being in Manhattan. I did not want to run into Slim on the streets of the Village. In the city, I'd spend all day obsessing over her, compulsively rewriting and printing out letters I would never send, arguing for her to reconsider. I used up an entire ink cartridge in two days and had piles of crumbled paper all over the floor.

On the last weekend in June, while gays in New York City marched and partied during the annual Gay Pride celebration, I took the train to Bay Head, New Jersey. I did not want to be in the Village that weekend seeing the thousands of happy gay and lesbian couples.

As I rode the shore local to the last stop, and the conductor counted off the beach towns…Spring Lake, Manasquan, Point Pleasant, Bay Head…I flashed back to another dramatic announcement: When I came out to my parents three decades ago in 1979.

My mother must have had some idea. The week before, she'd told me, "If you're going to tell us something upsetting, wait until after my birthday, dear." She put on her fake sweet voice that made me cringe. My brother, John, who already knew, had warned me: "Don't tell Mom and Dad. It will kill them."

But when he couldn't talk me out of it, he agreed to be there. He was late and walked in midsentence and stood listening in the hallway. "And I wanted to let you know, so I can be more open and we can have a better relationship," I said.

A framed picture of the Sacred Heart presided over the sunny kitchen with its tin ceiling and linoleum floor. Dad sat at the head of the table underneath the picture. Mom was at the other end; they were in their usual seats.

My father turned to me and calmly stated, "I think homosexuality is against the order of nature. It's abnormal, unnatural, deviate." His blue-grey eyes were enraged, like that time years ago when I was small and he grabbed me by the shoulders and shook me for lying about climbing over the fence into a neighbor's yard. Yet now he was furious at me for telling the truth. But I should have expected this reaction. My father was a formalist who followed the law of the Catholic Church explicitly.

For a moment, I felt stunned. But I recovered, caught my breath, and continued. "What do you think, Mom?"

"Well," she hesitated, searching the face of her husband of forty-some years, "I agree with your father, but you're still our daughter. And we still love you."

"You mean, even if I'm a deviate?" I asked sarcastically, as John slid into the table, eyebrows raised, and lit a cigarette. He seldom smoked inside.

"This news does not change our feelings for you," my father agreed, spinning his line on the "love the sinner, hate the sin" idea of conservative Christian thinking. "We still love you."

Although my announcement could have gone worse, I felt rejected and slumped into the wooden kitchen chair. They loved me, even if I was abnormal. But I wanted approval. They always sent mixed messages. I had pumped myself up for this and they dashed my hopes. But what else could I have expected?

Everything in our family revolved around religion. My parents decorated their turn-of-the-century house with statues of Jesus and Mary mingled with antique vases on wooden mantlepieces. As I squirmed, I looked up at statues of St. Anthony and St. Joseph who held dried palms twisted into crosses.

"I don't think I'm abnormal. Neither does my therapist."

"What would you expect her to say," my mother chimed in. "You said she's a lesbian, so she can't be objective."

"You're an adult," my father snapped. "You're entitled to your opinions, but we disagree."

My brother shook his head. He was on my side but did not interrupt our father. Why didn't he come to my defense? And what was he signaling with his hands? Look at the mess you started. They'd rather not hear this.

"Are you sure you're not just throwing this lesbian word around loosely?" my father demanded, staring directly at me.

"Why in the world would I do that?"

I was astonished at this suggestion. Months of role-playing in my therapist's office had prepared me for all kinds of possible parental reactions. Would they disown me? Offer to pray for me? Ask how I got this way? Try to turn me straight? When my shrink played angry father or distraught mother and I played the dyke daughter, the one reaction I didn't anticipate was having to convince them I was gay.

"Maybe you just haven't met the right man yet," my father said.

That remark struck me as funny. My father hated my old boyfriends from high school and college: Bob was a know-it-all. Joe was a druggie and effeminate.

"Perhaps this is just a phase, Kathleen, like when you were in a band and wanted to be a songwriter," my mother injected hopefully.

"Ma, I think I've been gay my entire life," I replied. "It just took me twenty-five years to figure it out. You must have had some idea, no?"

"Well, I did suspect this was what you wanted to tell us," my mother conceded, idly stirring the cold tea in her cup. "You haven't mentioned a man in years."

"But maybe you're just trying to be different," my mother continued. "You always were the nonconformist in the family, so different from your sister; you never cared much about honor roll grades in high school, never cared about—"

"Oh, Mom, please stop," said John, "that was years ago. Why start digging this up?"

"John, do not interrupt me," Mom said with a withering glance that reduced him to a baby.

"Then it was drugs in college," my mother recalled. "So maybe gay is the next thing? Is this the middle child syndrome?"

"My God! How much do I have to spell this out? Libby was my lover. Remember her? And my old college boyfriend Joe? Guess what? He's gay too. And I could think of much easier ways to be different. I can't believe you're bringing up high school. I felt out of place and depressed most of the time."

I was on a roll now. "Then I went to college and got stoned and drunk so I could fake it with men. My life stunk until I came out. I'm happier now because I'm being myself. I know I'm not the daughter you expected," I sighed, "but this is me."

No one spoke for a minute. John lit another cigarette, offered one to me, even though I'd quit last year. I accepted. This was hardly a typical day.

I glanced at the green plastic clock on the wall above the church calendar. That month, the Virgin Mary was being assumed into heaven by a host of angels. How I wished a spirit would come and whisk me out of this room. I had just endured the longest twenty minutes of my life and the scene was not over.

"Kathleen, your father and I do not deride homosexuals. We even had some gay friends in our day—witty fellows, everyone knew—but what your father and I don't understand is why you must label yourself and tell everyone."

"Mom, this isn't the 1940s. Next year is 1980. Gay people don't want to be in the closet anymore—like in your day. It's not healthy. Haven't you heard of gay liberation? Society won't change unless people come out."

"Well, what with murder and rape so common today," said Dad, "I don't suppose that homosexuality should seem strange."

John and I locked eyes. Did we hear our father right? Dad was a religious man, but he was intelligent. He had been educated in Jesuit colleges. Why was he comparing my lifestyle to that of the lowest criminals?

"Dad, I really don't appreciate being lumped in with murderers and rapists," I retorted, "with people who are evil." I had forgotten how mean my father could get when he was upset. I was disappointed my mother let him, but she feared his disapproval.

"There's nothing wrong with being gay," I shot back, ready for another round. All that practicing with my therapist had paid off.

"Kate, can you please stop here for today?" John intervened, sensing the growing antagonism and sounding scared. "Mom and Dad are on information overload."

By now my mother was crying and talking about some article she saw in *Ladies Home Journal*, "My Daughter Is a Lesbian." My father was scowling under the picture of Jesus Christ as I said goodbye, put on my jacket, and left to catch the next train to Hoboken.

My parents and I never really talked about my being gay after that pronouncement, and it's partly my fault. My father asked me to get him some books on the subject. I went to the Oscar Wilde Bookshop on Christopher Street and picked up *Now That You Know*, a parent-to-parent book, written to help parents accept a gay child. The other text was a Christian perspective on homosexuality by a gay priest. I never gave my father the books. I guess I didn't want to discuss this anymore then. I threw the news of my being gay out there, and then I ran.

Shortly after my announcement, I met Slim, and we wrote my parents a letter telling them we wanted to be accepted into the family as a married couple. Though I never felt our relationship attained full recognition, we were included in all major family events.

After my father died in 1999, my mother became more open and accepting. She made comments about how gay men were sensitive. She admitted the Church was sexist. Dealing with the next generation and their values forced her to change. Since she wanted her grandkids and great-grandkids at her dinner table, she had to accept that my niece was not raising her sons Catholic and my slacker nephew was living with his girlfriend. One time, when we discussed a magazine article, my mother mentioned that she'd had a good sex life after fifty.

"Too much information, Grandma," said my niece, blushing.

My mother had come a long way over the years, but I was still uncertain what sort of reception I'd receive to my breakup news. When I announced that Slim left me, I was sitting in the small living room of our summer house. My family was concerned and got it, even my elderly mother. My adult nieces and nephew added their generation's perspective.

"You guys were together a long time," said my mother. "It's just like getting a divorce."

"Yeah, but without being entitled to anything," I added bitterly.

"This is why gays should be able to get married," said my niece.

"That sucks, but you're a strong person," said my surfer dude nephew.

"Maybe she'll come back after she gets this out of her system," said another niece. "Mom had a friend whose husband did that."

My niece, who is psychic, told me privately, "Kate, I'm very sorry, but not surprised. Last Christmas, when we were at the dinner table, I sensed Slim didn't want to be there."

No one in my family said anything negative about her, which surprised me. They just felt worried and badly for me that this was happening. It was so comforting to have their support, and I knew this was where I'd be spending time this summer.

The weather was rainy that first weekend when I told my family about the breakup so my mother suggested we visit some yard sales listed in the local paper. How weird to be doing this activity with her and not Slim. I slipped into the driver's seat of my mother's old bomb because I hated the way she drove, one foot on the gas pedal, the other on the brake.

We rode a few miles to Ortley Beach and turned on the street listed in the ad, but the numbers did not make sense. We saw signs with arrows, but when we followed them, we got lost.

"Where is this stupid sale?" I said, realizing I was so upset that I should not have been behind the wheel. I made a hasty K-turn as we tried the street again. "This was your big idea," I snapped at my mom.

"Let's give this one more try," said my mother. "Maybe the numbers go the other way. Or the signs got turned around."

"That's it," I said, in frustration as we went up and down the street again.

"Okay, forget it. Let's go to the A&P. I need to pick up some groceries."

The supermarket was a couple of blocks away. I took off in a huff. As I pulled into the parking lot, a police car followed me into the lot.

"Oh, now what? Just what I need this weekend."

I parked the car and waited while the officer got out and walked to the window. Mom was rummaging in the glove compartment for the registration and insurance info. I undid my seat belt so I could grab my wallet from my back pocket and get my license.

"Hi, officer. Why did you pull me over?" I knew I was not speeding.

"You went through a stop sign on that corner," he pointed a block away.

"Sorry. I didn't see it," I said honestly. "I don't know this area," I lied.

He took all the info we handed him, gave my mother back the car forms, then went back to his patrol car with my license. Luckily, I had a clean record.

"This is your fault," I said to my mother. "You insisted we find that sale. Then I got all flustered on these stupid little streets. He's gonna give me a ticket and I'll get points—and—"

I knew I was being obnoxious to my mother but I was totally upset.

"I'll pay for it, " said my mother as the officer came back to our car.

"Well, Ms. Walter, I have decided to give you a ticket for not wearing your seat belt. I'm giving you a break so you won't get points, but be more careful in the future. There have been some accidents at that corner. You can pay this online by credit card."

"Thank you, officer."

My mother kept her word and sent me a check for the ticket, along with a note. "Better luck next time we go to garage sales. Keep well. Better days are coming, Love Mom."

During July and August, I hopped the train at Penn Station to the Shore on Tuesdays and returned on Fridays, so my nieces and their kids could take over the cottage on weekends. When my mother picked me up at the train station in Bay Head, I filled her in as we drove to our house.

"Have you heard anything from Slim?" she'd ask each week.

"No." I'd shake my head, trying not to cry.

"Geez, that's pretty rotten, after all these years."

One week, my mother had her own Slim story. She told me how she mistakenly dialed Slim's number, apologized and quickly hung up. "She sounded really sad," said my mother. "Even when she said hello, it was a sad hello."

So she was sad too. I wasn't sure if knowing that made me feel better or worse.

I was depressed in the city but found comfort staying in the family house and sleeping in my childhood bedroom. I got into a routine. During my two daily bike spins—morning and evening—I rode the length of Bay Boulevard, three miles each way, looping around West Point Island. In the afternoon, my mother and I went to the beach. We sat side by side in our chairs holding paperback novels.

Although in her mid-eighties, Mom went into the ocean every day in summer, even when the water was freezing. She enjoyed swimming but needed help getting in and out of the water. Everyone knew her; she was the only person on our beach who wore a bathing cap. Mom was short, barely five feet tall, but she still looked good in her flowered one-piece suit. One day I was holding her hand at the edge as she dragged me into sixty-degree cold water. "Come on. It's great once you get yourself all wet."

Since I'm much taller, I was hopping around in waist-deep water while she had already immersed herself. "Chicken, chicken," she taunted playfully, as onlookers laughed from the shoreline. Mom splashed water on me, "Go under, get wet."

I dove under the next wave; it was like ice. I resurfaced, yelling, "It's freezing. I can't believe you dragged me in here."

Now we were both laughing. I swam around a bit, adjusting to the water, recalling how she was the parent who years ago had taught me to swim.

In the evenings, we read some more. Her chair was in a corner in the living room; mine was in the alcove. I'd glance up and see her. As we sat in the house, surrounded by the faded knotty pine my father installed, my mother told me reading helped her after my father died. When we tired of books, we played Scrabble. One night, as I made the word "eros," I realized this was the longest I'd gone without sex in my adult life.

When I went to the Jersey Shore I felt like I was on vacation from the breakup, since Slim seldom came to our beach house when we were together. But the loss hit me hard when I returned to the city. I could not call her the minute I walked in the door, as I always did, and say, "Hi sweetie, I'm home." When I checked my email, there was no message saying, "Welcome back. I missed you." I was all alone in my apartment. I used my shrink and friends to help me decompress from my mother and used my mother to help me deal with Slim.

Once again, I saw how Slim and my mother were alike. The traits that initially attracted me to Slim were the same ones that drove me nuts. At first, I loved her take-charge attitude, but after a while I felt Slim was too bossy, like my Mom. While straight girls often "marry" their father, I had married my mother.

But there were differences: Slim got crabby whenever I was sick. My mother was kind and concerned when I was not feeling well. My recent breakup seemed to bring out those caretaking qualities. My mother related to me better when I was needy and dependent.

I always felt competition between Slim and my mother for my love, and I clearly stood up to my parents more after we became a couple. I told my mother that she was overbearing and picked on me for being independent. She immediately started to cry, repeating the line, "We loved you all equally." I hated when she turned on the waterworks. It felt manipulative. She was a weepy person, crying over sad movies on TV. Whenever I fought with Slim, I too became agitated and weepy.

Spending time with my mother, I could see where I got some of the traits that annoyed Slim. Like my mother, I was compulsively industrious, flitting from one activity to the next. My mother reported aloud while reading the paper on the beach. I did the same thing at home. Mom had an amazing ability to whitewash family problems—rocky marriages, substance abuse, mixed up grandkids. Like her, I had whitewashed my conflicts with Slim over the years.

At the shore house, Mom played social director, hovering over me, planning my day, suggesting joint activities. If I were outside talking to a neighbor, she'd jump into my conversation from behind the screen door. If I pointed out this was too much and not relaxing, she got upset. She couldn't see me as separate, just like I had trouble separating from Slim.

One day, we were on the beach under the umbrella in the shade and she suggested, "Why don't you move your chair into the sun?" as if I could not figure out this option myself. She wondered why I got exasperated with her and said, "All mothers are bossy."

Another time, when the two of us were talking, catching up on family news, I thought she had a keen mind and lots of energy for her age. I was glad I had good genes.

My mother was a control freak, yes, and I doubted that would ever change, but my trauma brought us closer. She was keenly interested in the details of the break-up and the aftermath and concerned about my emotional health. For years, I kept trying to get my mother to really see me, and it finally happened. Maybe her widowhood helped her empathize with how much I was suffering from the loss.

"You'll have days like that," she'd say when I told her about a bad spell. She was becoming a role model for grieving. If she could survive the loss of her husband of fifty-seven years, I could get through my gay divorce. How funny that it took losing my lover to reconcile with my first love—my mother.

The beach house was decorated for fall; the shell lights in the bay window had been replaced by strings of pumpkins. An entire season had passed without contact with Slim. At this point in my life, our summer cottage felt like the safest place in my world. My mother puttered around in a pink sweat suit as she turned up the TV too loud. That drove me crazy but I didn't say anything. She really liked watching *Jeopardy*, but then she shut the tube off and we settled into our reading chairs.

The sunrise brunch on the last weekend of October was the finale of the season at Ocean Beach. I had never attended before and figured that was a good reason for one last visit. People gathered around a bonfire to watch the sunrise and drink coffee, then retreated to a neighbor's house for a sumptuous brunch. The invitation said rain or shine.

It was raining when I got off the train on Friday evening with blustery winds predicted for the next morning. I was not prepared with my jeans jacket and down vest, and needed better gear. After dinner, my mother got up from her reading chair and suggested we look in the beach closet for rain jackets. I stood nearby as she started going through a bunch of communal mackinaws stored for foul weather.

"Try this one," she said as she tossed out various hooded parkas. "Or this one."

I settled on a blue jacket with a plaid lining while my mother tried on a green one. I had to help her into it because she has arthritis in her hands.

"Too tight," she said as I assisted her out of the green and into a brown.

"That looks good, " I said to my mother, as I waited with my hands shoved into the pockets of my borrowed garment, trying to adjust the snug fit.

"Okay, I'll wear the brown," she agreed.

"Ick. What's this?" I asked. The inside of one pocket was all sticky. "Who wore this last?"

"Oh, the boys used these jackets during the hurricane last month," she said, referring to my great nephews. "They had so much fun."

"No doubt eating candy while they watched the storm."

"So sure, we're all set for the morning," Mom said, evoking a mock Irish brogue, something she never did, as she closed the closet and walked back to the living room.

The next day, my mother knocked on my door a little before seven. The wind was howling and rattling the windows.

"Will the bonfire be on?" I asked. "Seems nasty out there."

"Well let's walk to the beach and find out," she said.

I got dressed quickly and we left the house. It was pouring and too windy for umbrellas or a bonfire. I ran ahead and got to the beach first. It was empty.

"Forget it," I said, as I headed back to the street to meet my mother. "Is it too early to go to the brunch?"

"We'll go back to the house, get the coffee cake I made, then go over there."

The aroma of freshly brewed coffee hit me as soon we entered the neighbor's sun porch. Bacon was frying and the kitchen counter was filled with bagels and cream cheese, quiche, muffins, cakes, fruit salad, orange juice, and champagne. I'd known the hosts since I was a kid and introduced myself to the faces I did not recognize. I grabbed a coffee and bagel and settled into a living room chair next to my mother who was chatting with a friend her age.

"Why don't you sit with the other young people," she said, referring to a crowd of folks in their forties and fifties who were mingling on the sun porch. I rolled my eyes at her pushy suggestion. I hated being treated like a child, but I realized that in her eyes, I'd always be this spunky outgoing little girl, a tomboy who hated wearing dresses.

4

THE AFTERMATH: FALL 2006

Slim was sexy, a cool dresser, and a fantastic dancer. She was smart with a good sense of humor, down to earth and not pretentious. Until the breakup, I'd considered her loyal, trustworthy, and dedicated. She made me feel loved and special with the mushy notes she wrote in my greeting cards. She gave me sound career advice and supported my writing.

She was calm and confident, a good balance to my excitable nature. I always felt she "got" me and I could be myself with her. If we went to a party and met someone new, we could tell just by looking at each other's expressions, that we felt the same way about this person. We had similar musical tastes and loved dirty dancing in the apartment to funky music.

When I hadn't heard anything from Slim by the end of September, I emailed her about getting back my art deco lamp and my fall clothes still in her closet. The woman with three closets bursting with garments wrote back that she had been wearing my green military jacket and wanted to keep it. She claimed she originally gave it to me because she thought it was too masculine for her but didn't feel that way anymore. Was she turning from femme to butch?

She concluded by saying she hoped I was okay and knew it had been difficult. "Difficult" was an understatement. I'd lost sleep for months and dropped twelve pounds. It was the most traumatic loss I'd ever had. One day I was crying so hard in the shower I choked on the water. What had happened to the woman who slow danced with me not that long ago to "Strangers in the Night" on New Year's Eve?

Slim had made it clear in the note that she couldn't have contact at this point and wanted me to respect that. She had to protect herself first (from those pesky feelings she still had toward me?) It seemed bizarre, after a quarter of a century together, to not sit down and have a postdivorce conversation about finances and friendship.

She wrote, "I wish the best for you and am concerned about your well-being." That line seemed disconnected from the way she was acting. I couldn't believe the woman who had always helped me through bad times was gone.

I didn't have the strength to argue about my jacket, which looked good on me. But I had to retrieve my aunt's heirloom lamp. So Slim packed it carefully and dropped it in my lobby, along with a few other items. Since she'd refused to let me inside the apartment to look around and gather my belongings, I later recalled other things I'd forgotten to request, including a framed vintage drawing of a European street scene that I'd hung in all my living spaces. Now it was hers, which seemed wrong.

After retrieving most of my possessions, I sent Slim a three-page snail mail letter explaining what I thought had gone wrong with our partnership. I felt sending it might give me closure. "I'm so sad that you have to shut me out and keep things separate in order to feel like you're not going to lose yourself," I wrote. "All couples struggle with intimacy, but you don't have a handle on it. You're so afraid of being dependent that you cut off your needs to be close. You always fled from examining your feelings—and lots of repressed feelings got stirred up by that sex toy. This made you feel angry and out of control and I got blamed."

This was not just a breakup; it was a life quake. The future I'd expected had been ripped away and now my life had big cracks. We always planned on getting old together in Westbeth Artists Housing, after I eventually got a bigger apartment. We'd be two aging bohemian dykes, like my upstairs neighbors. Slim promised we'd get married if it became legal in New York state.

We were giddy that day in 1993 when we registered as domestic partners at the Municipal Building in lower Manhattan. Since the bill had just passed, the place was filled with gay and lesbian couples, and the clerks were in a jovial mood, congratulating everyone. Slim's hand was shaking as she signed the form. Upon leaving, we had our picture taken by the city photographer, who handed me a fake bouquet and a "just married" sign. Although a New York City domestic partnership document only offered a few local benefits, it felt as significant to us as a marriage license. I never thought we'd end up like the 50 percent of broken heterosexual marriages.

Of course, in the eyes of New York State, my marriage to a woman was never a legal bond. When I consulted a Fifth Avenue attorney, who specialized in gay and lesbian couples, he said I had no rights. I learned the hard way why legalizing gay marriage is important.

As a freelance writer and adjunct instructor, I lived frugally but never made enough money to save. Slim made a lot more than me (from reselling news photos), and her savings were to be our retirement income. Slim had natural talent, an aggressive drive, and she was a good businesswoman. She made the "ka-ching, ka-ching" cash register sound after she negotiated a photo sale on the phone, laughing at how she could make $500 in five minutes.

For years, we lived with a darkroom in our tiny kitchen. After she went digital, she often asked for my input when editing pictures at the computer. I helped her pick photos for contests and wrote funny captions. When a major outlet stopped using her, I pushed her to attend a press conference, which resulted in her regaining the client. The stability of our relationship created the synergy to make her a successful photojournalist. She acknowledged my role when she wrote, on our twenty-fifth anniversary card: "My career as a photographer is forever dedicated to you." (Reading her tribute made me cry.)

After two and a half decades, I didn't think I should walk away penniless. If we'd been legally married there would likely be some formal contact, and we'd be getting together our affairs during this hard transition. I could hand my lawyer a list of items and he could negotiate for them. More important, my lawyer could argue for equitable distribution of her IRAs and many savings accounts. My name was listed as beneficiary, but not being married, I had no legal claim to the money unless Slim was dead. This six-figure nest egg was earmarked for our retirement, and I had led my life believing this would be there for me. Slim always told me not to worry that I made less because she would take care of me when we got older.

For more than a quarter of century, I naively lived with no legal protection other than her will. Now I was alone and panicked about my future. I was dumped, emotionally bereft, and left in a fragile economic situation with only a few thousand dollars in my bank account. When I'd emailed Slim to ask about a share of the retirement money, she never responded.

I woke up in the middle of the night worried about becoming a bag lady or having to live with my siblings in suburban New Jersey in my later years. Would I have to leave the Village and move into the apartment my brother created in his house for his aging mother-in-law? Or would I have to move in with my sister into one of my nieces' empty bedrooms?

Ironically, this tragedy turned me into an advocate of gay marriage. I always thought of us as two hip downtown dykes, too cool for that stuffy institution. But now I realized marriage provided protections that I never expected to need. How funny that a Greenwich Village lesbian couple could turn into a cliche of a middle-class American heterosexual marriage. I'd played the sensitive female role, stoking the sex and relationship fires. Slim was the stoic male breadwinner.

"If you think you'll get a settlement out of guilt, good will, or doing the right thing, forget it," said Lexa during a post-breakup reading. She noted that Slim's actions were no different from straight people's, and that's why we have those laws, which unfortunately didn't apply to unmarried gays and lesbians. "Money is symbolic," she said. "You're focused on this because you want restitution. Drop it—if you turn this into a grudge, it will prevent you from moving on."

I wondered if I was fixated on the retirement money as a pathetic way to stay connected. I was still exploring the sorrow and would need to ride this through for at least a year. There was no quick fix.

Everything was harder without Slim. When something good happened, I wanted to call her to celebrate. When something bad happened, I wanted to call to commiserate. When I organized a big political meeting on a controversial neighborhood issue, and everyone said I did a fabulous job, I wanted her in the audience to watch me in the spotlight.

But I refused to stay home and mope. I went to concerts in the park, readings, and panels. The yoga institute and the gay center were on the same West Village block—a ten-minute walk from my place. If I had to be a middle-aged dyke who was dumped, at least I lived in a great neighborhood for single lesbians. I checked out the Cubbyhole, the local lesbian bar, although I stopped that when I realized most of the regulars drank too much.

The November after the breakup, I was in the East Village when I saw Slim walking just ahead of me on Second Avenue. I hadn't seen her on the street since April.

"Hey, Slim," I called out and she turned and stopped. I had no idea how she would react to me but I couldn't let this opportunity pass. Looking at her, I was shocked. She looked like she had aged six years in six months. The lines in her face were deeper, her cheeks were sunken, her skin was sallow, and she had more grey in her hair.

"Slim, you don't look good," I blurted out, as if we were still together and I had the right to scrutinize her. "You're too thin. You've lost more weight."

"I was exercising too much this summer," she said, "but I stopped doing that. I'm not sleeping well," she admitted.

"That's because you miss me," I said and leaned over and impulsively kissed her on the lips. I couldn't resist. She was startled, but did not flinch. "What's been going on?"

"I've been hanging out with friends," she said.

"Like who?" I asked, upset she was hanging out with anyone but me.

"Uh, I don't want to get into that," she said.

By now we were approaching the corner, where she was going to cross the street. This was my chance to ask what I was dying to know.

"Why did you completely cut me off last summer? That was so cold."

"I had to do it that way to move on," she explained.

I was tempted to say that if this was what moving on looked like, then maybe she should have stayed put. Instead I said, "Now that time has passed, can we talk?"

"You're the one who wants to be friends," she said snippily.

While lesbians are famous for remaining close friends with their exes, this was obviously too stressful for Slim.

"Any chance you'll consider therapy now?" I said, knowing this was a long shot.

"Nah," she said waving her hand, dismissing this idea as if it was crazy.

I was concerned that she looked like she was suffering emotionally. This was not just my impression. Slim looked exactly the way my friend Sara had described her when she ran into her at the end of summer. Sara said she barely recognized her.

We had reached the corner and I wanted to keep her talking, to make her stay. We'd walked down Second Avenue together hundreds of times and now she was going to cross the street and walk away—like I was nothing to her! Slim was the keeper of my history, the only person in New York who knew me when I was in my early thirties, struggling to get my byline into major publications.

"I've seen some of your recent photos. Great work," I said.

"Where did you see them?" she asked as if I were spying on her.

"Where do you think? In the papers and online. I saw you shot Annie Leibovitz. What was she like?" I asked, knowing her diva reputation.

"She was nice. She was fun and wanted to take my picture too."

Oh great, what was next? Would I read about them together in the gossip pages?

We were at the crosswalk and Slim was waiting for the light to change. I told her my niece had a baby girl in September and asked about Slim's parents. She said they were the same. Now she was ready to cross the street—my last chance. She had asked nothing about me. The Slim I loved for twenty-six years was beautiful and buoyant. She had been replaced by this tall gaunt figure sprinting away from me.

"Why are you acting this way—like a different person?" I said.

"People change," Slim said, walking away without saying goodbye.

I felt the universe brought us together for a reason. While it was true that the breakup was harder on me because she initiated it, my friends said that I "had suffered well" and looked good. It was distressing to see Slim appearing older and unhealthy, like something was eating away at her. I was stunned at how much Slim's personality and attitude and even her appearance had changed. Seeing her this way shook me up.

When I told my therapist about this encounter, Dr. R. thought the post-breakup situation seemed eerie. She wondered whether I had been a stabilizing influence who kept Slim grounded and she was adrift without me. The fact Slim appeared to be struggling made our breakup seem more tragic. I wished I could heal her, rescue her from herself, yet I couldn't even heal myself from losing her.

Though I missed the old Slim, I also felt relieved. Our relationship had become draining and it was demeaning to keep begging for crumbs of her attention for years.

Dr. R. encouraged me to look at my emotional masochism, a big dynamic in our partnership. What was I reenacting from my childhood? Why did I let Slim be the boss?

In that sense it was good we split up. I needed to have higher expectations in love and work. I'd worn blinders that enabled me to focus more on the good and less on the bad. I believed Slim when she told me no one else would put up with my annoying habits. The idea of dating again in middle age was daunting, so I always strived to fix things.

Years ago, when—at my suggestion—we went to into couples counseling because we were fighting a lot, the shrink said we had issues with power and control. It was funny and complicated, in a very lesbian way: Slim, the fashion-plate femme, was acting like a stereotypical man—cutting off her feelings and refusing to explore them. I was the soft butch, nurturing the relationship, acting like a stereotypical woman. Back then, Slim wanted me—the sensitive butch—to initiate sex, yet she was a bossy femme who insisted upon running the relationship. I resented doing all the emotional work, especially since I often felt powerless.

Although counseling was helpful, we left and slipped back into bad patterns. I hated her passive-aggression and found her incredibly provocative when she didn't own her feelings. She would begin an argument saying, "you did this" or "you did that" rather than saying how she felt or what she needed. Her communication style put me on the defensive.

But when we first met, I was the queen of ambivalence, and had loved her take-charge attitude. I lacked confidence in myself. It was reassuring that she was in control. But as I gained confidence, I started to buck under her reign and this caused conflicts. So I bent to her will, as I did with my mother.

I was the self-effacing Catholic schoolgirl married to a strong but beautiful Jewish princess. Slim was the oldest of three, a very bright child doted upon by her nutty parents. As the middle child of three, I was more used to adapting. I was afraid of being equal, that she'd get jealous if she was not on top. I was so scared of losing her that I'd become way too accommodating.

When my snoring bothered her, I slept on the floor in the living room because she refused to buy a bigger couch where I could stretch out. I took the cushions and arranged them on the floor. I put up with her watching television in bed when I wanted to read. I went along with her limited restaurant selections, so we always landed up in the ultraorganic Angelica. To give her the space she requested, I split my time between two apartments. We never had enough sex to satisfy me, and we stopped taking exotic trips once her career took off and she needed to be within range of her beeper 24/7.

I tried to make her happy, but got dumped in the long run anyway! The woman I'd devoted a quarter century of my life to had left me forever without even saying "I'm sorry."

I had sacrificed my needs to stay in the relationship because I loved Slim and I liked being part of a couple. Being in the relationship had made me feel safe, so I tolerated the stretches where I got little in return for what I gave.

Dr. R. felt this was tied to my family background and my father's religious fanaticism. A daily communicant at Mass, he needed to feel there was a higher power in charge of what happened in life. When I was with Slim, she was the higher power who made me feel safe and that things would work out. I put my faith in her.

The summer before the breakup, we were staying in a Bed & Breakfast in Ocean Grove, and as we went left the inn, dressed in sandals and shorts, Slim asked the owner for another room key, adding snottily, "Do you think we're tied together at the waist?"

I never felt that way but that must be how she saw our bond. I felt close but not merged, maybe because I had a stronger sense of identity. I was in analysis and taught personal essay writing. She had spent the past two decades developing an exciting photography career, but did little introspection. Then she woke up at fifty-two, seeking more from life.

Friends predicted that Slim might want to get back when she got this out of her system, but as I processed the breakup in therapy, I realized I wanted to share my later years with someone kinder and more nurturing. I knew that in the future I would not tolerate a lover who was not self-aware and analyzed. I had become more idealistic.

I had stayed with Slim because I loved her a lot. We were best friends and I was always turned on by her. Slim was at my side through difficult times, like when my father died. I thought we had enough good stuff to keep us going. We had stimulating conversations and laughed at similar things. After I'd invested so many years, I didn't want to walk away. I kept hoping she'd come around. I had gambled with my heart and lost—big time.

Lexa suggested getting back in touch with the radical lesbian feminist that I'd once been and ditch my inner housewife. I wasn't happy about being single at fifty-seven, but I knew my chances of meeting someone compatible were much better than if I were a straight woman. (Unlike fifty-something single men, lesbians didn't usually seek younger partners.)

My friends said I looked much younger than my age. (Must have been all that yoga.) Now I could meet someone more emotionally open and willing to do her share of the work. Expending so much of my energy trying to prop up my relationship with Slim hurt my career. I would not make that mistake again.

"There will be someone else down the road," said Dr. R., "and you could be happier."

"Love will come again," predicted Lexa.

Sending False Hope: Winter 2006. As the holidays approached, I was dreading Christmas without Slim. I was still too sad to buy a tree for my apartment. When I took out a box of old cards, at the bottom of the pile I found the greeting we'd sent two years earlier. Four cats were jumping out of a gift package and one looked just like our Tyler—blonde and fluffy. I was so upset I put the box back into the cabinet, wondering how would I get through this season.

A few days later, I went to get the mail and found an envelope from Slim. My heart lurched. It was a lovely card with dried flowers pressed into homemade paper. Inside was a handwritten note wishing me Merry Christmas and good health, peace of mind, and fun in the new year. I was confused and wondered what this meant. I sent back a short email thanking her for the card and including family news. I hoped her health had been restored (after the shingles) and that we could talk in the future. She wrote back thanking me for the email and wishing my mother a happy eighty-fifth birthday. Slim said her physical condition had improved, she'd be in touch, and the next year would be better for both of us.

"It's a big switch from the person I met on the street last month," I told my shrink.

"It's nice to learn she still has warm feelings," said Dr. R. "It seems like she misses you, but don't get your hopes up. She's opening the door a little, but to what, no one knows."

The holiday wishes made me feel good, as did the possibility of us talking and working on closure. I wanted to understand this more. It was hard to believe that Slim would not be sitting next to me at my mother's dinner table on Christmas Day, putting her hand on my knee under the table or standing next to me hitting the high notes when we sang carols around the piano.

This season I would be ringing in the new year alone.

5

GOING BACKWARD AND FORWARD
2007–2008:
LOOKING FOR ANSWERS

After the breakup, I kept searching for clues as to why. I'd walk past Slim's car parked on the street and peer inside for anything to explain her desertion. That approach yielded nothing, but the Internet was a treasure trove. What did I learn from Web Stalking 101, from googling her name?

"Courthouse News" reported Slim was suing Time, Inc for half a million dollars for copyright infringement of a valuable photo. Her credit was omitted from a book, and she hired a big-time lawyer. Her case looked like a slam dunk; now she'd make another pile of cash. This annoyed me. While her lucrative career may have been "forever dedicated to me," she left without any discussion of the retirement funds. Yet I had to take responsibility for being far too trusting.

I remembered the night Slim realized she had this hot photo of a mob boss with one of his lieutenants. We were home in the East Village sitting on the futon watching TV when a breaking-news story came on. Slim ran to her file cabinet of negatives and started jumping up and down, "I've got it. I have them together." Then I started jumping up and down too.

More discoveries from web stalking after the breakup: Slim had joined a bunch of Yahoo meet ups, social groups for lesbians. Many of them were private, and I wasn't interested enough to sign up and look further. It was easy to see what groups she was a member of since she chose not to hide it. Of course, all joining up meant was that you got notified about events. I noticed that she had a pattern of being more active with these groups after holiday weekends. *Lonely*, I thought. For this she broke up with me?

One group Slim belonged to was a table tennis group where she described herself as "open and honest." That self-description floored me coming from a woman who had withheld so much information about her sex life until we were breaking up.

Of course she went for vegan, vegetarian, and alternative health groups too. She was zealous about that stuff, always into the physical but not the emotional or spiritual. That's why it surprised me that she had also signed up for a meditation group. Was she trying to become more like me? The weirdest group Slim joined was about becoming a siren, a seductress. Her activity in these meet ups seemed to slow down around the same time I lost interest in her online activity.

For more than a year, I checked on her life regularly. In the beginning it was a way of hanging on and staying connected, but then I saw it as a small window into her new mind-set. One day I noticed she had added a head shot, a self-portrait. It was dark sepia toned. Slim was wearing a hat, like a fedora; she was not smiling and had this scary look in her eyes.

I still found Slim's photographs online on various news sites. I loved her shot of "the Renegade Cabaret," where a jazz singer performed on an impromptu stage on a fire escape overlooking the new High Line Park. It was twilight, the sun setting in the background, paper lanterns decorating the fire escape. The lighting in the photo was exquisite; she caught the singer in an expressive moment as the crowd watched.

In another search, I found a couple of essays she wrote about her work. Slim was a decent writer but I always had edited her. I remembered how we struggled with her 9/11 piece for "Digital Journalist." She felt guilty that she ran after the first tower collapsed. I thought that was a smart instinctive reaction. She deemed it cowardly that she did not return, even though the air was terrible. I helped her finesse this piece so her actions were understandable to colleagues. She could have gotten very sick had she remained.

Other than the big lawsuit, the weird photo, and the "open and honest" line, I didn't find anything shocking. My involvement was child's play compared to the frenzy Katha Pollitt described in "Webstalking," her personal essay in *The New Yorker* where she followed her philandering ex and his new girlfriend and all the women he fucked while they lived together. Reading this made me feel less obsessed and less abused. At least, Slim never cheated.

Pollitt had tried to break into her ex's email. I didn't have a clue about Slim's password. She once told me, "You'd never guess it."

My discoveries were minor compared to Pollitt's, but I totally agreed with her analysis of her web stalking: "It could mirror facts and events, but not only could it not control or change them, it could not answer my real question: Why?"

Returning to the Municipal Building. It felt sad to be alone at the Municipal Building among happy couples tying the knot—while I was there to get unhitched, to dissolve legal ties to the former love of my life. By the time I went downtown to file for my "gay divorce," two years after the breakup, I was well aware that domestic partnership in New York was a legal joke. I'd waited because I hoped Slim would return to her senses over time. But when I wrote her again, stating my case for financial reparations, she accused me of harassing her.

After that blow, I decided to officially dissolve my former domestic partnership. Since there were no real divorce papers to sign because lesbians couldn't get married in New York State, I needed some rituals to help me move on. But I forgot that everyone around me would be so gleeful because this was the same room where couples got marriage licenses. I was surrounded by brides in white gowns and cocktail dresses, men in tuxedos and suits. They anxiously waited on lines while best men clapped the guys on the back and joked about them finally making it legal. Little flower girls with bouquets ran around the dingy old office as family and friends waited to witness this happy occasion, which would take place in another room across the hall. I stood alone, watching them.

After I'd downloaded the paperwork from the Internet, I thought I had everything necessary. Yet, when I got to the correct window after waiting on two wrong lines, the clerk told me, "You must first send your former partner a certified letter indicating that you are dissolving your union and then come back with the form from the post office."

That procedure made little sense since the City Clerk would have no idea if the letter had been picked up or what the letter stated, only that it had been sent. I was tempted to send her a nasty missive but I restrained myself. The following week, I mailed a business-like certified letter, returned to the civic building and went straight to the correct line. The clerk examined my driver's license, accepted the form, photocopied the post office receipt onto it, and made copies. I wrote Slim's address on an envelope so the City Clerk could mail a duplicate. I signed the paper, she notarized it and then I went to the payment line with my credit card. It cost $27.00; plus $5.30 for the certified letter. The $32.30 for my fake divorce indicated how little our relationship was valued by mainstream society, although the ritual meant something important to us when we'd registered as domestic partners.

As I waited for the elevator and looked at my affidavit of termination, I felt dazed. It was so different from the day when we'd happily stepped out of the elevator doors to become partners in 1993. Now I was struck by the fact we had been together 13 years at that point and, it turned out, we'd lasted another 13 years.

I also noticed the date of dissolution was July 15, 2008. The number 15 is significant for me. My father was born and died on the 15th. I felt this was synchronicity, a sign from the universe. It seemed cosmically potent that I officially buried my past with Slim on that date.

I exited the building into a gorgeous summer day. Feeling relief, I decided to walk across the Brooklyn Bridge to take in the stellar view of lower Manhattan. As I turned around midway over the river, I was keenly aware of the missing twin towers. I recalled my fear that morning, terrified that Slim might have died in the building collapse. I had been so relieved when she called me crying and describing her narrow escape. We got closer after that scare. Now I contemplated what I'd had gained and lost since we'd parted.

I walked along the Brooklyn Bridge back towards Manhattan, hopped the subway to Union Square. Glad to be on familiar turf, I treated myself to a veggie burger at Village Yogurt, a lunch place Slim never liked. It was not organic enough for her. As I sipped my green tea, I was glad to eat what I wanted.

At home, I emailed several friends who congratulated me on my quick, cheap divorce.

"Hey, mine dragged out for years and cost thousands of dollars," a pal replied.

"Yeah but you got a house and a load of money from your ex," I kidded back.

I drank white wine that night and danced around my apartment to Tegan and Sara's new CD "The Con." The lesbian twins' quirky songs about love and loss seemed perfect for the occasion. I had long discarded the music Slim and I danced to together. Instead, I had a good cry to Mary J. Blige singing, "I remember when you used to love me." I wound up my private party dancing like mad to Bebel Gilberto's sizzling new samba, "Bring Back the Love."

As for my ex, I can't say I was surprised that the certified letter I was required to send her came back to me a few weeks later, "Unclaimed."

Back in the Pew. After Slim dumped me, I was looking for meaning beyond therapy sessions and psychic predictions. I was especially lonely on Sunday mornings, normally reserved for brunch with my lover. I craved structure to fill this empty space, and I needed spiritual cleansing from the negative energy of loss. So I started attending services at Middle Collegiate Church, a gorgeous old edifice on Second Avenue in the East Village.

Over the years, I'd visited this "hip" church for special neighborhood events (Slim and I went there on Christmas Eve the year before we split), but now I showed up regularly. I slipped into a rear pew and often cried when the choir rendered a poignant hymn, like "Amazing Grace." I stared at the beautiful Tiffany stained-glass windows depicting Biblical scenes, as I wondered why God was making me suffer like this. Even my ex had said I'd been a loving and devoted partner. I sought comfort from attending church again.

I'd been raised strict Roman Catholic back when nuns still wore habits and ruled the parochial schools that I attended from kindergarten through college. When I was around nineteen, my parents were crushed that I stopped attending Mass because my native religion seemed too conservative. My Irish-born mother cried as she pronounced, "You lost your faith." My father prayed for my return.

After I came out as a lesbian in 1975, I could not imagine going back to a denomination whose celibate leader proclaimed my sexual orientation a disorder. Instead of formal Sunday worship, I found spiritual solace through practicing yoga and meditation.

Before my "gay divorce," I'd made tepid attempts to reconnect with my old religion after staying away for decades. It seemed like something was missing in my life. But when I checked out two Catholic churches in Greenwich Village, what was once familiar ritual now felt distant. I needed worship services that were more spirited and that fit my downtown dyke lifestyle.

At Middle Church, where the motto was, "Welcoming, Artistic, Inclusive,

Bold," the arts were woven into the services and related to the liturgy. For Advent and World AIDS Day, singers and actors delivered a theater piece about an HIV positive pregnant woman on the Lower East Side. Every week was different. Modern dancers gyrated up the aisles and jazz combos grooved. A traditional choir rendered hymns and a gospel chorus rocked.

For Palm Sunday, the church presented excerpts from "Jesus Christ Superstar" with extra singers brought in for this special event. Some had Broadway credits. The first time I experienced this service, I walked home through the Village humming "Hosanna Hey" carrying my palms, recalling how I did this as a kid. But now the hosanna was, "I'm here. I'm queer. I'm Christian."

The congregation prided itself on being multiracial, multicultural, and gay inclusive. One Sunday, they introduced new members and a black M/F transgender initiate sashayed up the aisle to applause and a pastoral embrace. This felt like the church for me to get renewed. Suddenly, I felt in touch with my religious roots while also in sync with the adult believer I'd become since leaving behind rote recitation of the catechism.

Reverend Dr. Jacqui Lewis, the senior minister, was a charismatic preacher whose sermons segued from discussing Thomas Aquinas and St. Augustine to declaring "Jesus is in the house." This pastor's brilliant interpretations of the gospel were uplifting. A tall attractive black woman, Reverend Jacqui had everyone roaring the Sunday she unpinned her braids, played at smoothing her hair, and imitated Condi Rice, or the day she compared Luke's time-jumping gospels to the writing techniques in a soap opera.

"I like being pastor of a church that is being disciplined for its positions," Jacqui had announced from the pulpit in 2008. The minister was referring to the fact that her congregation was under fire from members of its parent denomination, the Reformed Church of America, because it came out publicly in support of gay marriage in New York State.

Jacqui was also a great dresser who alternated from ministerial robes to power suits or African garments with matching turbans. Her fashionable wardrobe and changing hairstyles caused gay men to gush as she walked onto the altar: "Oh my God. She looks fabulous."

Going to this ecumenical Protestant conclave soothed my soul—the music, the prayer, the sermons that rocked. When I visited their website, I discovered their creeds were similar to what I learned as child. I was back. After sitting in the pew for over a year, my attachment grew and I decided to become a member.

When I told my therapist—an agnostic Jew—that I was attending church I wondered how she'd react. "That's great. Whatever gets you through the night," she said, quoting John Lennon. My shrink thought the rituals offered a soothing structure that helped replace the relationship. I'd unconsciously elevated my ex into the role of my higher power, who made me feel safe and protected. So when my lover betrayed me, my life felt chaotic.

After the breakup, I kept thinking of the REM song, "Losing my Religion." Now I had to make the jump into having faith in myself, and to possibly finding a new practice. So the horribly painful breakup had one good effect—reopening my mind to religion, which I'd cast aside years ago. For that surprising blessing, I said, "Amen."

Joining Middle Church was easy. It involved two meetings with other applicants in Jacqui's office where everyone in our group described his or her religious background. To my shock, one older woman had been raised an Orthodox Jew on the Lower East Side. There was a gay male couple—one grew up Pentecostal, which he described as homophobic, and his partner was from a liberal Unitarian background. Another man with no religious upbringing found the church when he designed their website. An Asian woman had been raised Buddhist. Then there was me.

It was a safe bet that after Reverend Jacqui, I had the most knowledge of Christianity of anyone in the room. Religion was part of my Catholic school curriculum from kindergarten through college. I studied Latin for two years and earned twelve college credits in theology.

One of my concerns was whether I'd have to renounce anything to join Middle Collegiate Church. (Jacqui reassured me I didn't.) I couldn't imagine formally eschewing my background. I saw myself as an "expanded Catholic," grown in a new direction. I was definitely not converting to the Reformed Church of America, but I took this move seriously and wanted to be sure that it was okay to simply become a member of Middle Collegiate Church. (Jacqui said that was fine.) So I joined this renegade congregation.

Since this church had a large LGBT presence, I entertained the notion I might meet someone there. When I first started attending services and I turned to pass the peace to the woman sitting in the pew next to me, she said, "Weren't you Slim's girlfriend?"

I didn't recognize Kip until she reintroduced herself. She knew my ex from when they both worked out at Crunch gym back when it was located on St. Marks Place. Kip and her partner had broken up years ago. She was cute, a fashionable "lipstick lesbian."

As the rest of the crowd continued to greet one another, I filled Kip in on my breakup. After the service ended, she wished me well and asked if I came there often. The next time I saw her I asked her out for coffee and gave her my number, but she was not interested. Meeting someone at church would've been a nice fringe benefit, but that's not why I kept showing up week after week.

I never thought I'd resume regular Sunday attendance in late middle age, but joining Middle Church felt right. The services were like performance art. Reverend Jacqui radiated love and joy. I felt embraced, centered, uplifted, and less afraid to be on my own. This was my first step on my spiritual journey to healing and renewal.

Trusting My Vibes. Another post-breakup turning point was a weekend workshop at the Omega Institute in Rhinebeck, New York, in August 2008. I attended a seminar called "Trust Your Vibes" with Sonia Choquette, a popular spiritual teacher and prolific author. A former flight attendant, Sonia was perky and cute, a hip dresser in short, flowing skirts and bare feet.

Sonia started by telling the large audience, "We have a divine appointment to be here." I had discovered her in such a freaky, almost mystical, way that I was ready to believe in a "divine appointment." The previous summer I'd won a grant to take a writing workshop at Omega. By chance, Sonia was on campus the same weekend. On the bus ride back to New York City, everyone was raving about her course, so I decided to check it out the next year.

A terrific presenter, Sonia delivered her message about following your intuition through many personal anecdotes: one time she was driving to pick up her daughters from school and had a strong feeling to turn in another direction She followed her hunch and rescued a toddler who'd escaped from a negligent babysitter and was wandering around the streets.

Her running theme was that everyone can learn to "trust your vibes" and move from living in a five-sensory world to a six-sensory world, one informed by intuition (the inner teacher). I loved her analogy that being five-sensory was like having an analog television and then being invited to go digital, into a higher frequency. Loving life and raising your vibes would help manifest your goals. "Sad sacks don't create," Sonia said, which made sense to me.

A Catholic school grad, she cited Jesus and Buddha as major influences. She called herself an alchemist and a psychic, a trait she inherited from her Romanian-born mother and a gift honed from a young age. Sonia led us through exercises where we expressed our fears, what held us back. We got into pairs and one person listened intently while the other kept repeating, "If I wasn't afraid I would…" and then we switched. It felt cathartic to say, "If I wasn't afraid I'd be more adventurous and travel again. If I wasn't afraid, I'd be more spontaneous."

I wanted happiness and peace in my life. I wanted to sell my book. Sonia was giving out practical tools to make good stuff happen. Her confidence convinced me I could do all this.

At one point she quoted Einstein: "The intuitive spirit is a sacred gift; the rational mind its faithful servant." She noted we had thrown away the gift and become enslaved to the servant. As she reminded us, we'd all had intuitive experiences, events we called synchronicity. I thought of how I'd kept bumping into Slim on the street. Did that mean our vibes were still connected?

"You can't learn this intellectually," said Sonia, who told us not to take notes. "It is about surrendering and giving yourself permission to go to another realm. The root of this new paradigm is to not be controlled by the ego, whose vibration is low, dark, fearful. Divine Spirit rides on a higher wave. We have to welcome it back and we do that by trusting our vibes."

Music and dancing played a big part in creating this vibrational shift. I was chanting and gyrating to drums as we left our seats to dance and feel the spirit. I loved dancing and now I was moving to my own drummer, getting into the groove without a partner.

The workshop also involved getting in touch with our breath through exercises, like deep, three-part breathing. I realized I was already on the path, with an established breathing practice. I did yoga and meditated daily. I loved dancing around my apartment. Going to church fit into Sonia's message about tuning into the Source. All my practices were coming together.

Meditation always felt natural to me. In the seventies I took yoga classes and learned TM (Transcendental Meditation). My practices fell off when I moved to New York. I picked up meditation again when I resumed yoga in the nineties (as an antidote to aging), but now I used a different mantra.

Sonia was a kind and funny teacher who'd expanded into an author, inspired by her friend, the writing guru Julia Cameron. Of course, Sonia used that story as an example of how to manifest your dreams. When we returned from an afternoon break, she signed the two books I had bought at the Omega gift shop.

I felt like a different person as I got back on the bus that Sunday afternoon—bolder, less afraid. I was moving forward, determined to become more joyful and intuitive and go deeper into this realm. I started to believe I could manifest what I wanted if I stayed faithful to my intentions.

PART TWO

6

EMERGING INTO THE LIGHT:
JUNE 2009

After suffering for three years following the breakup, I emerged from the darkness a different person. Once a cranky journalist, I became a New Age optimist. Now here I was walking through my studio apartment twirling a lit smudge stick, making sure the pungent scent of sage got into every corner. I popped *The Best of Enya* into my CD player and pranced around to the Irish singer's ethereal sound and called upon my inner Celtic goddess.

I had always been intrigued by spirituality. But my interest lay dormant while I lived with a cynic who was grounded in the world of five senses. "I don't believe in that stuff," Slim said years ago when I interviewed Lexa for an article and tried one of her spells as part of my research. Without Slim's judgment, I now felt free to explore new areas. It was also a way to spite her ghost.

I can't say exactly when I plunged into this pursuit full tilt, but joining a church set the stage, and the weekend at the Omega Institute rooted me on this path. When I returned from upstate, I joined Six Sensory New York, a monthly group related to Sonia's teachings. I wanted to socialize with like-minded people.

I learned about the law of attraction, whose basic principle is that thoughts have an energy that attracts parallel experiences. I applied this in various areas of my life, and even in a bad economy, I had success in creating prosperity, so I became a believer.

I'd recently secured a coveted full-time job and my income increased. I went from being a starving writer and part-time instructor to full-time college teacher with a cool office that had a river view. While the whole country was in a recession, I was thriving. I didn't miss the irony in that twist, but I'd always been out of sync with the majority. During the eighties, when everyone was making tons of money, I was struggling to pay my bills. In the nineties, when lesbians finally discovered casual sex, I was monogamous.

Now everything was going well, except that I wanted a girlfriend. But working the principles that had brought me money (focusing on my intentions, doing creative visualization, keeping a gratitude journal, writing affirmations) had not attracted anyone special into my life. Looking back, I decided why the exercises in the relationship area had not materialized love and romance.

The books I'd devoured warned that negativity lowers our vibrations and prevents magnetism. In order to raise my vibes and attract a woman, I had to move past my anger. I was making progress on this in therapy. My shrink said I felt "safer" with the negative feelings, but the negativity created a wall. "You have a guard rail around your heart," she pointed out.

Lexa, my psychic, told me, "Love is there as soon as you want it. You're delaying it because you'd rather brood. Make your upcoming big birthday one of liberation." Turning sixty, I decided to go for it.

After the workshop at Omega, I'd immersed myself in New Age books like *The Secret*, *Soul Love*, *The Soul Mate Secret*, *Tune Into Love*, *Expect a Miracle*, and *Love Will Find You*. I compiled lists: the qualities I wanted in my partner, the things I'm grateful for, the attributes I like about myself, my interests and passions. I placed one list in a red envelope under my pillow; burned another list and tossed the ashes into the Hudson. My notebooks were filled with lists and affirmations that I recited, reminding myself that I was smart and funny and talented.

I chanted mantras in Sanskrit, built a small altar and bought crystals. I placed "my desire" on the prayer list at my church. I listened to guided meditations about finding a match. I hooked up to a machine connected to a laptop that printed a color picture of my aura. The results were no surprise: vibrant in the intellect, weak with intimacy.

On a physical level, I prepared my apartment, making sure I had at least two of everything—two wine glasses, two coffee mugs, two end tables. I went through my closets and shelves and gave away clothes and books. I put fresh flowers in my apartment and moved objects around, but only so much feng shui was possible in a 400-square-foot studio.

I cut up magazines and made a vision board containing what I'd like in my future. On a sheet of cardboard, I pasted pictures of sexy women and cupids shooting arrows and words like "sizzling city girl," "pleasure," "sacred sensualities." I added my own photo to the collage and pictures of the cool places my new girlfriend and I would inhabit—beach house and city loft. I kept moving the board around until I found the best location in my apartment.

Once I began exploring these methods, I got compulsive. I didn't feel silly about the exercises and obviously had lots of company in the New Age community. I knew the message in *The Secret* was basically a gussied-up version of the power of positive thinking—a concept that's been around for ages. Of course, landing a coveted job gave me confidence and having money made me less tense, more magnetic. I felt competent, powerful, independent. While I was interested in attracting romance, I was more invested in finding inner peace after so much turmoil, but they seemed to be connected. Still I felt I had to have myself together first, and later realized that I *needed* to create things in this order.

Dropping the anger remained a challenge. I still cursed out my ex on occasion, but I no longer did it every day. Instead of "bitch bucket burning in hell," I chanted, "She's coming. She's coming," a reference to my future mate who I pictured waiting in the wings.

I started going to dances and parties and fund-raisers, although the New Age authors indicated that our meeting might be quite unexpected. We might lock eyes in the checkout line at the health food store or the changing room at the yoga center. More than one psychic had seen me hooking up with a visual artist or someone connected with galleries. "Go to openings," they said.

I visualized delightful scenarios with my new girlfriend: she was sitting across from me at breakfast after we made love for hours. We were strolling in the river park or walking in the surf on a quiet beach. I admit that part of me laughed at my antics as I reeled through my apartment with the smudge stick like a possessed woman who had inhaled acid-laced fairy dust. But I believed I could make my dreams happen. I'd become shameless in my quest for love and romance, willing to try almost anything.

I stayed ready by eating well and doing lots of yoga, and dropped to my lowest weight in years. I even got a new hairstyle from a hip Chelsea salon. I ditched brushing my hair back away from my face and started growing bangs and combing my hair forward. Now I walked down Hudson Street and the world appeared full of potential.

Could my mystery woman be the "dark-haired, dark-eyed lady" I met at a workshop and ran into a few weeks later at a gay women's party? She seemed sexy when we danced to "Rollout," Labelle's latest hit from the group's first studio album in thirty years. If Labelle could make a come back, so could I.

The Reading: September 2009. Roland was reading my tarot cards in a café on Christopher Street. A large gay man with a pleasant face and booming voice, he reminded me of *Pavarotti*. The comparison was not a stretch since they had similar coloring, but Roland sang in Broadway musicals. I'd met him a few weeks before at the Spiritual Salon in East West Books. An acquaintance who ran the salon, told me he was her psychic. That impressed me since she herself was a gifted medium. Roland picked a corner table by the window. The place was empty and there was no chatter. I hoped my tape recorder would pick up his voice over the background music coming through the speakers. He didn't want to order until we finished the reading.

He started with a small layout and began to interpret: "The cards are saying that the strongest issue in your mind right now is finding a relationship and you're struggling. I do see somebody but it's not happening at the moment because—" He paused.

I was sitting on the edge of my seat anxious to hear more.

"You need a period of rest and rejuvenation," he said.

That made sense and I'd heard that from others, but how long did I need?

"Also, I feel like there are certain blocks," he continued, "that are not being addressed. You need to remove them to open up the pathway to this person."

"What are the blocks?" I asked, eager to blast through them.

"First thing I feel is some fear standing in your way."

Roland then dealt out more cards and said, "Okay, it's a water sign woman.

That's come up twice already, which means Pisces, Scorpio, or Cancer. What sign are you?"

"I'm Capricorn and so was my ex."

"So you were both earth signs. I have feeling this new woman will be a Cancer. This relationship is definitely coming in. Now what's the obstacle here?"

He studied the layout some more. "I'm going to go out on a limb and say that you are dealing with this on your own." He took a deep breath and put out more cards.

"Okay, here's what just happened," he said. "The card of being stuck got covered by the card of success through control, through dealing with your emotions. I keep feeling like you're scared to make a move."

"But I'm going out," I protested.

"Yes, but I see a blocked heart." He pointed to the cards again and showed me two horses going in slightly different directions. "Continue to go out because this is what's happening now and what comes next is a relationship, a very healthy one."

"Well, I had a bad breakup," I explained. "I was totally betrayed. She didn't even meet anyone. Just dumped me and cut me off completely. My shrink thought she broke up with me in the most painful way possible. To this day, I don't get it. That's why it's been so hard to recover."

"This all makes sense now," Roland continued. "No wonder you needed time to mend."

"Yes, other people have told me this is a sacred period for me to get myself together but I feel like I should be over it more—it's been three years. I'm still angry and wonder if that's a problem."

"You're allowed to be upset, and I don't think that is the block. What I see is that you are the one who decides when this recovery period is over—it's up to you. "

"I guess I'm afraid to be open after what happened," I said, feeling like I was talking to my therapist, not a psychic I had just met. "I don't want to get hurt again."

"Listen to me," he said, "this next woman that comes in—not only does she help you heal—but she's a past-life soul mate. Now let's talk about how you address this situation and tame the fears with love."

Roland indicated that the card of Strength had to do with taming the wild beast of fear—the picture showed a woman with a lion in her mouth, like it was her pet.

LOOKING FOR A KISS

"Look, it is a wonderful, scary animal but she's got control over it. It's normal that you would be fearful after what happened, but this person is coming in—it's definite, not a maybe—so be aware of the tendency not to go far enough. Try to be open."

I told Roland I'd had a few first dates but no second dates. I enjoyed dinner with a cute shrink but later heard through the gay girl grapevine that she was afraid to date a writer for fear that I'd write something negative if we got involved and broke up—talk about projecting!

Another woman, also a shrink, emailed me about how much she related to my two lesbian breakup pieces in a local alternative weekly. She even drove two hours from Connecticut to my reading at a club on the Lower East Side. Now that's the way to a writer's heart. I saw potential and we emailed for a while. But she decided she lived too far from me for dating.

I called up the woman who I danced sexy with to Labelle. When I asked her out to dinner, she changed the subject. I thought she was interested, that we had a moment, but I must have read her wrong. I was out of practice: the last time I was single, Jimmy Carter was president.

During summer vacation, I was attracted to this yoga teacher, who lives year round at the Jersey Shore, but decided not to pursue her when I discovered she was afraid of New York City, my beloved home.

Nothing had clicked, but Dr. R., my trusted therapist, who'd been with her female shrink partner for three decades, told me I was making progress.

She was right—at least I was allowing myself to feel attracted, and even if I hadn't met anyone yet, I was happy and busy in my reconstructed life. I didn't need anyone to make me complete. But it would be nice to have a sexy companion.

"You know what," Roland said decisively. "You are going to meet this person through a group and it starts off slowly. Oh, oh, this could be her." He pointed to a card with a king.

"It's a water sign and male, but sometimes gay guys come up as queens so a more butch woman could come up as a king."

I didn't tell Roland I was not usually attracted to butch types. I let him keep going.

"It happens the way you want it—this is a card of getting."

"Everything in my life is going fabulously, except for this one area—"

"I would challenge that," he shot back. "It is all going well. The wound from the breakup left you damaged—that's natural. When you decide you are done resting, when you are ready, that person will appear. It is not maybe—she does arrive.

"I'm telling you—all these cards are so clear—there is no question in my mind. So the issue is running forward and fighting your demons, that little fearful devil with soft control. Be gentle with yourself. Lower the stakes and just go out for fun."

I explained that I was not depressed, just frustrated at my lack of luck. He put out more cards and the water sign came up again—three times now.

Roland stopped and closed his eyes and said, "I'm getting stuff from the other side," and I guessed he was channeling spirit guides. He mentioned a dancer friend who injured herself and had surgery but was determined to go back on stage, even if in pain.

"So if I'm hurt, I need to take the risk and dance again," I said, enjoying this banter.

"Yes, then you will realize that you are not that blocked. My friend was in pain but she was so happy to be performing, she had tears in her eyes. The next night she took an Advil, danced again—and she got better. That's the way you need to look at this."

Roland analyzed why I was not meeting anyone. The imagery of blinders kept coming up.

"My shrink says I'm too critical when I first meet people. Could that be an issue?"

"Yeah, it's a defense mechanism, so you don't get hurt. But listen to me, she's out there. Do whatever you need to do to get to the place where you can welcome her in," he stressed. "The blinders won't come off until you get there energetically. So have experiences—online dating, whatever—that will lead you to be more receptive."

"But I thought we are going to meet in a group—"

"It's about the process of becoming open. I challenge anybody who has gone through pain to get this fixed in one leap—it's about taking steps."

I'd been devastated when my ex tossed me aside like a used tissue. Roland gasped as I relayed some of the details, "Are you kidding me? It sounds so painful."

As I was speaking, Roland started channeling again. "You have this person waiting in the wings right now. Nothing like the past will happen to you again. Your ex exercised her free will. She is exploring something with herself that has nothing to do with you."

"But why be so mean?" I asked, still struggling for answers.

"Did she have an anxiety disorder? I'm getting this panicky feeling."

"Well, she always had trouble sleeping."

"What is the panic, what is it?" Roland tried to get a handle, as he closed his eyes, waiting for more messages from his guides.

"She told me she felt life was passing her by and she wanted to see what she missed. All I know is that she turned fifty and started acting crazy. Maybe it was menopause."

"Like unfulfilled desires. Okay, here is what I'm getting now about the panic," he said. "I think she may feel she made a huge mistake."

"I'd never get back with her. I don't trust her."

"I'd scream at you if you even considered it."

"But it would be nice to get an apology. That would help me."

"Oh, you'll get an apology one day," he said immediately." I'll tell you when—when she knows you're with somebody else. I get that loud and clear. When you have somebody new, she'll come running back and you will see her differently then. Right now it's safe and comforting for her to know you are not with anybody."

"Like I'm here in the West Village and she is there in the East Village."

"Exactly. She knows where to find you. "

"Even though she won't speak to me," I added. "The other thing is that when I've run into her, like at a Q Girls dance in Chelsea where I'm with friends, my gay girl posse of the evening, we're having fun dancing, and she is always alone."

"Well, I'm telling you something is wrong with her. Did she have a problem talking in general? I feel like I'm choking," he said, putting his hand to his neck.

"Yeah, she had problems communicating her feelings," I said.

"Okay, so let's get back to you and what this is showing me." He glanced at the table and continued. At this point, I wasn't sure if he was reading the tarot or channeling spirit guides.

"The pathway you were on with this woman is done, and now there is a garden pathway full of light coming this way and a new love will be waiting for you."

"So many good things have happened to me that might not have happened otherwise," I said, knowing I was in a positive space now. Of course, I was not making a fortune in academia, and my new full-time job meant attending committee meetings where colleagues droned on about measuring student learning outcomes. Yet I was fortunate to land a coveted position teaching remedial English classes at an overcrowded community college. Now I had more income but less time to pursue my goal of becoming a book author. It was a trade-off, but I needed to take care of myself and plan for my future after getting financially screwed in the breakup.

I explained to Roland how I'd become a spiritual and self-help junkie, paying psychics and teachers for reading and workshops, devouring books on intuition and synchronicity. I meditated every morning. I worked on my yoga shoulder stand posture and breathing practices and attended church regularly.

"I've been taking hatha yoga classes for many years," I said, "but after the breakup I got into the more spiritual aspects of yoga. I read the *Yoga Sutras* and started chanting."

"You're on the path," he assured me. "Clean out the dark thoughts with love." Roland recommended a chakra cleansing CD and suggested I practice unblocking my heart chakra.

"All my friends tell me I'm doing well and look great," I said.

"Your energy feels good, but look at this," he pointed. "This card here represents you. See how her eyes are covered and swords are all around her. Swords represent the mental chatter that keeps us from action. They are energy blocks. Releasing them can be difficult."

He took one more look at the cards. "I think that's it. We're good."

I thanked Roland, paid him a modest fee ($25), and we went to the counter to order cappuccinos. As we scooted back to our table, sirens wailed on Christopher Street. It was a warm late September night and still felt like summer.

During my walk home, I thought about my long strange trip, my spiritual journey. I went from being a nice Catholic girl from an observant family to a yogini who practiced hatha yoga (asanas or postures, like the sun salutation) and bhakti yoga (chanting of the names of the Hindu gods in Sanskrit.) I had joined Middle Collegiate Church, a radical congregation in the East Village led by a charismatic black female minister.

I now considered myself interspiritual, blending Hinduism with Christianity, my core belief system. I started out praying the Mass in Latin and now I was chanting in Sanskrit and reciting the Protestant version of the "Our Father."

Three years ago, I was seeking meaning and consolation after the breakup. The methods I'd used as salves to soothe me through the hurt evolved into the components of a happy and expanded new life. That was a big surprise. My quest evolved organically and it was fun.

I'd come a long way from my parents' conservative beliefs, which ruled my childhood in New Jersey. My friends were shocked when I told them it was harder for me to tell my parents I was not a practicing Catholic than to come out to them as a lesbian (not that it was easy, but it was easier). I pulled up those roots and had little to replace them for decades, until the breakup when I reawakened spiritually and my inner spark caught fire.

While all this was happening, I was in psychotherapy with Dr. R., an agnostic Jew who applauded my renewed fervor. She knew me for decades. I did serious twice a week sessions with her in the '80s and '90s on the Upper West Side. My reconnecting with her during my big break-up was a life line. Never a fan of my ex, she said that I had "blossomed."

My spiritual journey did more than help me recover from an amputation: it delivered sustenance and filled a lifelong void that I struggled with for years in therapy. As a queer and feminist, I'd angrily ditched the sexist and homophobic Catholic Church decades ago. I was outraged when the pope (John Paul II) issued an encyclical that gays are disordered. During the AIDS crisis when New York's cardinal attacked condoms, I protested with ACT UP in front of St. Patrick's Cathedral with a big sign: "Keep your rosaries off my ovaries." But uprooting myself from a strict religious upbringing was wrenching and left a gaping hole in my soul that remained untended until I joined a new church as I nursed myself through trauma.

One day, while I was browsing through magazines left in my laundry room, I stumbled upon an article about resilient people. It felt like I was reading about myself. I had almost all of the characteristics: I was healthy due to regular exercise and a good diet. I had a thriving spiritual life. I was connected to family, friends, colleagues. I was generous, a trait inherited from my father, who gave so out of proportion to his modest income that he was audited by the IRS. (Luckily, he had all his receipts.) I had become optimistic, which surprised me.

The research even suggested resilience could be genetic. If so, I got that part from my mother, now an eighty-seven-year-old widow going strong, taking chair yoga and tai chi, and running two households.

The article mentioned what some shrinks called "post-traumatic growth syndrome." This was obviously what I had experienced after the breakup. The syndrome was defined as when an individual gains strength from adversity and converts misfortune into good luck and becomes a better person. Who knew there was actually a psychological term for my emotional growth spurt? Even Dr. R. never had heard this expression. Now I wondered how this process worked for me. Did having these traits make me resilient, or I had I became resilient doing these practices? Or a combination? Whatever the case, this idea rocked.

When I returned to my apartment after the tarot card reading, I ordered the chakra cleansing CD from Amazon, pulled the book *Queer Astrology for Women* off my shelf, and looked up my compatibility with the water signs. I was making progress, but I still had to work on releasing the blocked energy.

A few days later, when I played back the tape from the tarot reading, I was relieved that my machine picked up everything. But what freaked me out was that the background music seemed like a soundtrack. When Roland was talking about the new person coming into my life, the music was airy and jazzy, like lounge music, but when he talked about my ex, it was like a cacaphony. I recalled the music had switched from mellow to brassy but did not connect it with the topics until I heard the tape. No more cacaphony. I wanted the jazz.

7

THE SIGHTINGS: NOVEMBER 2009

When I whirled into the Out Professionals women's mixer at the Rubin Museum in Chelsea, I scanned the room, noticing the ancient tapestries that depicted various phases in the life of the Buddha. The last time I'd gone to a similar event, I'd run into Slim, who'd refused to say hello, even when she bumped directly into me and I greeted her. Slim was easy to spot because she was tall, almost five feet ten inches. The coast looked clear tonight and I went to the bar to get a beer.

I checked out the room again and saw my neighbor Janey with a couple of her friends whom I'd met before. I went over to their table, said hello, and was introduced to two other women. I was in a great mood since I'd just handed in a big curriculum development project that I'd been working on for two months.

Janey was a neighbor-friend who lived in my building. She fixed my computer and I fed her cat and got her mail when she went away. It was a good arrangement except she sometimes made annoying remarks when she came to my apartment, like the time she told me I should remove that framed photo of a street scene that Slim had taken because it might make a new girlfriend think I was still into my ex. I viewed it as art. Never mind that I didn't have a new girlfriend and didn't ask her opinion. Janey also got on my nerves with comments about how the options for meeting women were limited at our age.

"That is such a negative way of thinking," I chided her. "You are focusing on scarcity instead of abundance." If I was out there looking, others were too.

I had gotten to the museum late and the postwork event was winding down.

"Anyone want to go dancing at Q Girls?" I asked the group. For some reason, these unrelated events were often on the same night. I was hoping Slim would not be at the club since she was not at the museum. Everyone declined except Amy, an attractive woman I'd just met.

As we walked the few blocks from the museum to the club, I learned that Amy knew a friend of Janey's from yoga and Pilates classes. Amy was tall and blonde with a slender, toned body, a pretty face, and a great chin-length haircut. She was friendly and did art restoration. I guessed she was in her late forties. She called her teenaged son to check on him as we walked to the club.

The basement den was fairly empty when we got there—it was still early—but it would fill up, so we paid and entered. We got beers and found a couch and started talking. That's when I learned she was bisexual, married, and still lived with her husband and son. Okay, so we'd just dance and have fun tonight. I'd never consider anyone who was bi and/or married. Let the bi women play with each other.

While Amy was telling me she had recently discovered women, and her husband knew where she was tonight, I saw Slim walk into the club.

"Oh no, my ex just entered," I told her.

"Which one is she?" Amy asked, looking toward the door.

"Tall, dark hair. She's wearing black sweat pants with a stripe."

"Was it an amicable breakup? Are you friendly?" she asked.

"No, she won't even speak to me," I said, recapping the breakup story quickly.

"Well, I don't like that," said Amy. "Do you want me to pretend to be your date?"

"Yeah, that would be cool," I said, smiling as Amy moved closer to me.

Slim had committed a cardinal sin. In the relatively small lesbian world where women were known for remaining best friends with their exes, she was not even courteous in public. Slim definitely saw me and retreated to the other side of the room, and I pretended to be staring intently at Amy.

"Did you say your ex had striped pants. Is that right?" Amy asked to confirm and I nodded. "Well, she is so checking you out. Her head keeps swiveling, like she can't stop looking."

I loved it. I'm sure it appeared like I had a date with this hot blonde yoga babe who was at least ten years younger than I. Amy and I chatted easily. She was into art and I lived in an artists' housing project with its own gallery. She was enthused when I told her I was a college professor and writer. I answered the requisite questions about where I worked and what I wrote: "creative nonfiction."

"This music is boring," Amy said. "Everything she plays sounds the same."

"I don't like this either," I said. "I wish she'd stop this techno shit and spin something funky."

The women sitting next to us were also complaining.

"Maybe we should talk to the dj," I said. "Give her some requests."

"She won't listen," said one of the women. "We tried that last time."

Just as she said that, I heard something I liked. It was old Madonna, so Amy and I got up and danced. Across the floor, I saw Slim dancing with this woman I knew slightly who was a vegetarian activist. She seemed nice, but struck me as plain-looking, with a terrible haircut and bad eyeglass frames. She had zero sense of style unless you counted her '70s butch look as so retro it was hip. Slim was a fashion plate who collected vintage clothes. Were they on a date?

Amy and I sat down after the dj resumed the boring music. That's when I looked up and saw Slim slow dancing with the vegetarian activist. But the weird thing was that it was not a slow song. As this grandstanding continued for several minutes, I had to wonder if she were showing off for my benefit.

I felt amazingly detached: no jealousy or anything. Let her dance slow with the bad haircut girl. I didn't care, not like when I ran into Slim here the first time, shortly after the break-up.

I'll never forget that night, which I now refer to as "The Return of Elvis." I was sitting with an acquaintance and saw two tall women dancing. One stood out because she was wearing this garish white/tan outfit with white bellbottoms and a glittery vest. In her outlandish costume she looked like a cross between an Elvis imitator and John Travolta in *Saturday Night Fever*. I was only ten feet away but had no idea who the woman was until I started dancing with this cute woman and someone rubbed my arm. It was Slim, in drag as Elvis/Travolta! Was she trying on different personalities? What was next? Michael Jackson? As I said hello, she gave me her smirky smile but said nothing.

I was shocked and my heart started beating so fast that I almost fell over. But I kept dancing and managed to finish the set. Afterwards, I returned to my seat, wondering if Slim would come over to talk to me, but she never did. So why did she touch me?

Thank the goddess I was much calmer this time when I saw Slim at Q Girls. Amy and I got up to dance again to Prince, who I really like. But when the music went back to techno, we decided to leave. When we went to retrieve our jackets, I saw Slim and the vegetarian sitting on the next banquette right next to our stuff. I cooly leaned into the couch and stared at Slim, grabbed my leather jacket, turned, and left with the hot yoga babe. I hoped it looked like we were going home together.

We walked a few blocks and hugged and said good night at the corner of 14th Street. Amy had volunteered to be my beard, a fake date. But what if Slim had a real one? Was she making more progress than I?

I had been putting off reading through and shredding all the cards and letters that Slim had sent me during our twenty-six-year relationship; I was not the type of person to just toss them out; I needed to wait until I felt detached enough, and now I finally did.

The morning after running into her at Q Girls, I pulled out a wicker basket from the bottom of my closet and removed an overstuffed envelope that contained over a quarter century's worth of birthday, anniversary, Christmas, and Valentine's Day cards, together with random notes. I kept a few cards to remind myself that this relationship had actually existed. All I had left were the cards and photographs.

Slim had written that the relationship was the foundation of her life and the thing she was proudest of creating. I still couldn't believe she destroyed it. Not only destroyed it, but totally cut me off and acted like we never existed. She did send me a card the birthday after the breakup and said she'd be in touch, but same as with the Christmas card, she had never followed through. Sending false hope seemed worse than no card.

As I kept reading and shredding and crying a little, I felt a mix of angry and sad. I still had trouble taking in her stunning betrayal. All I could think was that if anyone read these repeated themes echoed over the years (love, passion, devotion, commitment) and then learned about the way she had left me, they'd be very puzzled. Slim recited that commitment theme up until the breakup announcement, which she lacked the courage to do in person. (That news deserved more than a phone call.)

After the shredding, I went to the monthly meeting of Six Sensory New York, which reinforced the concepts Sonia Choquette taught at the Omega Institute. Local leaders had taken advanced training with her. That fall, we had a new co-leader, a perky blonde who had just moved here and used to run Six Sensory Denver.

The purpose of our meetings was to continue raising our vibrations and become more intuitive. The group met at a yoga center and we did different exercises. Once we played psychic charades. (We didn't act out anything; we just thought about the name of a movie and people tried to read our thoughts.) Today we were doing a shamanic journey, which I'd already done at home, so I knew what to expect.

Taking a journey involves closing your eyes and listening to repetitive drumming and seeing where your mind goes. Depending on instructions, you might begin the journey with a specific goal, such as meeting your spirit animal or meeting some guides. Or you could ask yourself a question and see what answers emerged.

The facilitator suggested focusing on a question as she handed us rattles. Naturally, I had Slim on my brain. We sat on the floor in a circle and listened to the CD that came with Sandra Ingerman's instructive book *Shamanic Journeying*. As the drumming started, we closed our eyes and began shaking our rattles. Unlike other journeys, I did not see or meet anyone, but after about ten minutes, I heard this statement clear as day: "She lost her soul."

In my next therapy session, I was eager to discuss this cathartic weekend with Dr. R. I told her about my running into Slim and not being fazed, about reading and shredding the cards, and about taking the journey and getting that message.

"What does it mean that she lost her soul?" Dr. R. asked.

"It means she is not the person I knew and loved," I replied, recalling how after the breakup Dr. R. had gently told me that, but it did not sink in at the time. Of course, I still did not understand how such a radical transformation could happen.

We spent the rest of the session talking about dating, a subject we had not broached in some time. The truth was that when I went out I was more focused on going to workshops or other events that were spiritually elevating, as opposed to specifically gay events. I felt that if I could raise my vibes enough, I could draw my new partner into my orbit, anywhere. I recapped what the psychic reader had said about needing to take off the blinders and open my heart. I was working on that through listening to guided meditations.

Dr. R. connected the two images. "You wear blinders as a way to keep your heart closed. Your heart is not open because you are afraid of trusting again and getting hurt."

Of course I knew I was afraid of getting hurt again after all the suffering I experienced. But then Dr. R. came up with some new insights.

"You are afraid of losing your hard-won independence. You don't know how to be independent and dependent in a relationship."

She noted that I was overly dependent on Slim and could not go as far as I wanted as an independent person. "You were a baby when you met her." (I was thirty.)

Dr. R. pointed out that I'd become so focused on keeping Slim happy (not an easy task) that I'd spent a huge amount of energy on the relationship. It zapped me and took away from my own work. I recalled how the psychic I saw in Woodstock had called her "the draining one" and I later nicknamed her Drano.

"But why is she slow dancing with someone and I'm not?" I asked, frustrated.

"Maybe it's easier to do that if you've lost your soul," Dr. R. said, without missing a beat. "This is going to be an interesting new year for you," she continued. "You are learning so much, including how to open your heart and not lose your identity."

"Well, at least I never lost my soul," I amended. "If anything, I got more in touch with it after the breakup."

I told Dr. R. that I felt happy and content, not lonely, but there was a missing piece.

"The ability to be happy on your own without somebody is a big achievement," she said. I thanked her for the compliment and made it clear that she was a great therapist who had a lot to do with me getting to that place. Then she thanked me.

"There is a lot going on," I said.

"Yes, it's complicated, with all these different facets," she said, "but it's good."

"Thank God I'm no longer obsessing and compulsively seeking clues," I said. "It took me a while to stop that craziness on the web," I recalled.

"Yeah, I was worried about you," said Dr. R. "But you're in good shape now."

At the end of November, when I went to see Dr. A., my eye doctor, I complained about eye strain at my job where my sight constantly shifted from text book to the classroom. I thought it was my glasses and expected to be issued a new prescription.

After doing all his tests he told me, "You have lost so much vision in the right eye in the last ten months, you might want to have the cataract removed now."

That shocked me. I knew I had a cataract in one eye, but the last time I was there he was adamant about my not needing surgery yet. I had no idea things could change so fast. This made me feel old—old and alone. I thought I'd do this procedure a long time from now, like when I was retired or when I had a new girlfriend who would pick me up at the hospital after the procedure. But the truth was I could not see well from that eye and my night vision sucked.

By the time I left his office I had scheduled the surgery for mid-January during my semester break. As I went online and looked at the procedure and got the visual of a veil being removed from my eye, I kept thinking about what Roland had said in the reading about taking off the blinders.

8

HOME ALONE ON NEW YEAR'S EVE:

JANUARY 2010

Unlike in the past, I had no plans for New Year's Eve or New Year's Day. Since I had no desire to go alone to any of the four women's events in Village bars, I'd decided to do my own thing. Normally I didn't care about going to a party by myself, but not on this date. I had no one to kiss at midnight.

My mother called me early that evening, thinking I'd be out later. She was on vacation with my sister and two nieces and their families. As she held the phone up I could hear them screaming in the background, "Happy New Year." Then she put on my adorable three-year-old great-niece who recited, when prompted, "Happy New Year, Aunt Kate."

I stayed home, made myself a nice stir fry, drank some Gavi, an Italian wine I love—white and dry and not sweet. I listened to music and bopped around my apartment. The wine had mellowed me out and I was glad I could enjoy dancing alone.

If I did say so myself, my tastes were hip for a sixty-year-old, and I was a pretty good DJ. I sang along with the harmonies from the Brooklyn indie bands Grizzly Bear and the Dirty Projectors. I slinked around to Antibalas, a funky Afro pop group from Bushwick. Then I grooved to the hypnotic sound of Oumou Sangare's new CD. I'd been a fan of this Nigerian singer for years. I capped off my evening singing and swinging to the soulful sounds of Sharon Jones and The Dap-Kings, also based in Brooklyn. The music scene had migrated across the river, unlike in the 80s when I covered artists at CBGBs, The Ritz, and Folk City.

LOOKING FOR A KISS

I was a little sad when the ball dropped, but that lasted two minutes and then I started singing "New York, New York" along with Sinatra, thinking how I love the city and being a part of it. I love walking around my cool neighborhood with its tree-lined cobble-stoned streets. I love going to uptown museums and concerts in Central Park and comedy shows at a queer theater space on the Lower East Side. I love going to readings and being part of a community of artists.

I cringed when I heard Dick Clark's slurry poststroke speech. He seemed so old, which made me feel old. I wanted to remember him as that young man from *American Bandstand*. I used to race home from school to watch that show and learn the latest moves. I'd gone from doing the mashed potato and the pony to taking African dance classes.

One more emotional icy patch and then I was skating into 2010. Slim and I always celebrated January 2—the day we met—as our anniversary. This year marked thirty years ago that we had clicked.

It was a snowy Wednesday night, the week after New Year's Eve in 1980. The woman I had been dating had just dumped me. My new year's resolution for the new decade was to join more political groups—a better way to meet someone than the women's bar scene. Call it fate. We met at a gathering neither of us had ever attended before.

The monthly meeting of gay and lesbian teachers was packed because the guest speaker was Sandra Feldman, the dynamic president of the local chapter of the United Federation of Teachers. At this time, New York City did not even have a gay rights bill to protect us. The chairs were all taken, so people were standing or sitting on the floor. I spotted Slim leaning against the wall.

I thought it cool that this tall, dark-haired woman was wearing white cowgirl boots that made her two inches taller, almost six feet. After the meeting, the fags went to some male bar and the dykes went to the Dutchess. By chance, Slim and I landed up sitting at the same table.

I liked her immediately. This woman was not a phony—she was a native New Yorker, glad to be home after a trip to Los Angeles. The conversation flowed easily. She lived in Soho, had just started teaching, and was also working on her master's degree. She grew up in Brooklyn, but her parents now lived on Long Island. We danced fast to Donna Summer and I saw she had original moves. I had three beers to her unfinished one. We left the bar together, exchanging last names and phone numbers on scraps of paper, and trading quick hugs. Jewish, I thought, when I saw her last name.

I could not get her out of my head. I screwed up my nerve and called and asked her out to Sunday brunch. She said she had been trying my number too. No one had answering machines. I was still using a typewriter. We agreed on a place and I tried to recall her face. I was not disappointed when she opened the door of her apartment. Slim was so pretty—black hair, brown eyes, beautiful complexion, delicate features, and three inches taller than I.

After brunch at the Broome Street Bar, we took a long walk through the Village. I did not want the afternoon to end and thought she felt the same way. We walked west to the Hudson River and onto the funky queer piers. It was cold but not windy, a clear winter day. She wore mittens and I cupped her hands in mine as we sat huddling together. Back then, I was the one with a camera and I took shots of Slim with the World Trade Center looming in the background.

Still not wanting to part, I went back to her place. We smoked a joint and Slim put on the Crusaders' new record, "Street Life." During our six-hour first date, I was fascinated to learn that Slim had married her high school sweetheart, who had come out a couple of years before. I told her about me and my college boyfriend, Joe. I thought it interesting that we'd both been involved with gay men who were Italian and who remained our close friends. Slim was still just coming out. I had been a dyke for five years but then again, I was five years older. I had good feelings about her right from the start and I was determined to win her over.

Our second date was on my thirty-first birthday. We went to see "Gertrude Stein, Gertrude Stein," a one woman show at the Provincetown Playhouse. I had scored the tickets. Then she treated me to a late dinner at an Italian bistro. I was smitten, and as we finished our meal, I asked Slim if she'd like to come back to my apartment. She agreed. Whenever we reminisced about that night, we'd laugh about how I had stocked up on breakfast in advance—with the hope that I could get her to spend the night.

Slim was sexually shy and would not let me go down on her, so I just used my fingers. I wondered if this was because she had not been out long. I vowed to be patient, but knew this would not work unless she became more sexually relaxed. After two more dates, I got the go ahead.

We fell hard and fast in love and moved in together a few months later, abandoning our places for a sunny one-bedroom walk-up on St. Marks Place in the East Village.

I also recalled our twenty-fifth anniversary five years ago. We had a sweet evening at home as we toasted our quarter century together with sparkling cider and chocolate cake. I gave her an anniversary card with a note enclosed: "25 reasons why Kate loves Slim." She handed me a blank card with a heart and "our love" on the cover. I cried when I read what Slim wrote about feeling blessed to have me in her life.

Slim gave me a beautiful close-up shot of us, heads cuddled, my arm over her shoulder. She'd taken it a few days earlier, holding her camera at arm's length. The picture was in a lovely white frame with a ribbon in the corner. We were smiling, happy together.

Since it was a warm January evening, we decided to return to the spot where we clicked in 1980. We walked over to Sheridan Square where the Dutchess once stood. The space had been through several incarnations since the popular women's bar closed. This night, it was empty and undergoing renovations, which made it easy for us to recreate the old scene as we peered inside through the glass. The layout was the same with the bar in the exact spot. I could almost see the women sitting on the stools, their heads turning whenever a new face entered the room

"The tables were in the back," said Slim pointing to an empty area beyond the bar.

"What if we hadn't sat at the same table?" I asked.

"The entrance looks a little different," Slim observed.

"You were standing right there when we walked in from the gay teachers meeting," I said, pointing to the foyer, "leaning against a cigarette machine."

As I said that, I pictured Slim that night in her blue jacket and shoulder length black hair.

"Let's walk to the corner where we hugged goodbye," she said.

"I'm so glad I had the nerve to ask for your number," I said as we headed toward Bleecker Street.

"Me too. I can't imagine how different my life would have been had we not met."

"I can't either."

As I went to bed reminiscing about how we met, it hit me that the location where I'd snapped her picture on our first date was basically the same spot where Slim, the photojournalist, took my author photo right before we broke up. Of course, now the World Trade Center was missing from the background.

9

I CAN SEE CLEARLY NOW:

JANUARY 2010

To get this decade off to a good start, I'd decided to do the 21-Day Consciousness Cleanse, a three-week program of emotional detox and spiritual renewal. Based upon the best-selling book by Debbie Ford, the plan devotes a week to contemplating past, present, and future. It seemed like a perfect way to end an intense decade and start a new one, and I wanted to go inward before the eye surgery. The 21-Day Cleanse involves lots of journal writing, answering questions, and writing letters to yourself.

I began the program a few days earlier than the new year, on December 27th, my parents' anniversary. My mother had told me she was writing out her wedding invitations when she heard on the radio that Pearl Harbor had been bombed. She felt scared and wondered what it would be like to marry and raise a family in this uncertain world. A devoted couple with longevity, they were a hard act to follow. I'd never get to spend over half a century with the same person.

As I wrote out the journal pages for the cleanse, I started thinking about this awful past decade (the big breakup, 9/11, Bush) and I realized how for me this horrible period started in 1999 when my father died and ended in 2009 when I got my new job. So in my head, I was already one year into the new era.

I always spend the last day of the old year and the first day of the new one doing meaningful things I want to continue doing in the future. On December 31, I took a yoga class and during the balancing poses, I focused my gaze on a bare tree outside. Snow covered the deck furniture in the Manhattan backyards, creating a tranquil scene. We ended with several breathing practices. I had finally advanced with my alternate nostril breathing to the point where my exhales were longer than my inhales. That had taken years to master.

New Year's Day, I got up early, had coffee and oatmeal, meditated, did the journal writing for the 21-Day Cleanse. Turned on my computer and read a long funny happy New Year's email from Bob, my first serious boyfriend; he and his wife were travel book authors. Bob was a really funny guy. He sat behind me in homeroom and got me in trouble laughing at his wisecracks about this ancient nun who refused to retire. We caught up at our high school reunion and ever since then, we emailed several times a year. Bob was a direct link to my straight past.

It was a mild winter day with no wind; the temperature was in the forties, great for a walk in Hudson River Park. I loved having nature only ten minutes from my apartment. The day was so mild, I went to the end of the Christopher Street pier, which was blissfully quiet.

I looked west across the river at New Jersey, my birthplace, and started chanting softly "*Lokaa Samastaah Sukhino Bhavantu*," which translates as "May the Entire Universe Be Filled With Peace and Joy, Love and Light." I chanted and turned north, east, south, west. I did this three times in each direction. I was sending out good vibes to the universe and the region and my home for the new year. From the pier, I could see Westbeth, the building where I lived.

I went back to my apartment and as part of the cleanse's Day of Desire, I made a new vision board, sparser than the old one (which had not worked). This one was simple, more like a map on a pretty background. I covered the cardboard with flowery wrapping paper and I added only two pictures (an attractive woman in the cross-legged meditation position and a cute lesbian couple in bed laughing). To get the photos and slogans for the board, I sat on the floor cutting up a lesbian magazine and a New Age catalogue. On the left-hand corner the slogan read "The Future Begins Now." On the bottom right corner, underneath the photo of the two women in bed, I pasted "The Courage to Love," "Wet for Her" (in big bold lettering), and "Soulmate Attraction: Calling Your Life Partner."

While I was finishing up week one of the cleanse (the past) I did a ritual where I shredded a bunch of photos of Slim and me together (I still had a whole boxful). That night when I went to open up my convertible couch, it jammed and I could not budge it. The sofa bed had been giving me trouble for weeks but it died that night. I did not think it was a coincidence since Slim had bought it for me. I had left the past and she was in the past, and the couch she gave me was no good any more.

I was happy to have a good reason to replace it, but now I had no bed. So I ended up sleeping on the floor after I managed to dislodge the mattress from the half-opened frame. I had to yank out the mattress in sections because the couch no longer opened up fully. Then I shoved the now uncomfortable couch back into place. In the cleanse, I was into week two and approaching the Day of Humility. Perfect timing. I was crashing on the floor in my tiny studio and sitting on a lumpy, broken couch.

As I watched the news footage from Haiti and saw the total devastation, it was hard to feel sorry for myself. I went on a cleaning binge and mopped my floors since I was sleeping there and didn't want to get any dust in my eye before or after the operation.

I didn't sleep well the night before the surgery, not just because I was scared but because I had to get up very early to be in the hospital at 6 A.M. I was awake before my alarm rang. I got dressed and did three rounds of *kapalabati* breathing, also known as the yogi's cup of coffee. I was dying for a real cup of coffee but had orders not to eat or drink anything.

During the twelve years I'd lived in the far West Village I'd never walked around at this hour; it was still dark and super quiet, like a transition period between shifts. All the restaurants and bars were closed and the stores hadn't opened yet. It felt a bit spooky. The only place open was the 24-hour deli at Abingdon Square. I grabbed a cab, easy to do at that time, and we shot across 14th Street to the Eye & Ear Infirmary.

I sat around for a while until I entered the presurgery assembly line: admission, hospital garb from the waist up, then a battery of eye drops that widened my pupil and numbed my eye. As I sat on a gurney in the hallway, waiting to be wheeled into the operating room (I had never been in one before), I started practicing alternate nostril breathing, a nerve-calming breath my yoga teacher recommended. I did not care if the hospital personnel thought I was weird. It helped me relax.

While in the corridor, I met the Filipino nurse and the anesthesiologist with a Russian accent, who'd be assisting my surgeon. Dr. A. came by to say hello. "Are you anxious?"

"Of course," I answered, hoping I would not be the rare patient whose retina detached.

"You'll be fine," he said and patted me on the shoulder.

The entire thing took less than ten minutes. All I remember was the needle going into a vein in my hand and staring into this bright light. I heard Dr. A. say three things: "The cataract is out. This is going swimmingly. The lens is in."

I liked the adverb "swimmingly." When I heard that word, I felt secure. Although I was sedated, I felt very aware. I left the OR with a clear plastic patch on my eye, but my distance vision was amazing. My friend Janey had come to pick me up in her car. I felt kinda high when we left the hospital—a mellow high. When I got back to our building I was shocked to see the lights in my hallway were bright white, not yellowish. I wondered if having better eyesight would allow me to envision new possibilities.

The following week, when I felt better, I went to the East Village. I was still connected to this neighborhood where I'd lived for twenty-two years. Compared to the supergentrified West Village (my current home), the East Village was funky, with more restaurant choices for vegetarians. I liked to walk around, see what was new, what had closed, and what was still there, although I avoided St. Marks Place, where I had lived with Slim. The block was still busy, with many cheap fast food places, but it had changed a lot from when we'd organized a block association to fight the crack dealers and the illegal peddlers brazenly selling stolen goods they'd ripped off from local apartment robberies.

I took a quick look at the sale table at St. Marks Bookshop, and then I went to Veselka's, a landmark Ukrainian restaurant thriving for decades on Second Avenue. After a hearty winter meal of vegetarian stuffed cabbage with mushroom gravy, I called my DJ friend Stan, whose studio was a few blocks away. He was home and invited me over to listen to some new mixes.

Stan lived in a tenement without an intercom, so he had to throw the keys from the fire escape. As I stood outside the building, I called him from my cell phone to let him know I was there. I was looking up waiting for him to step out when, to my shock, Slim appeared in front of me on the sidewalk. Her hair was more gray. She said, "I recognize that hat."

LOOKING FOR A KISS

I realized I was wearing a black vintage ski cap she gave me. I was stunned and said, "Yeah, I still wear it sometimes."

Stan came out onto the escape and threw a mini-football with the keys stuffed inside a carved-out slot. I was focused on catching it. I hated when I missed and the ball bounced into the street. I caught it, but when I turned around, Slim was six feet away, taking off. She waved to Stan and was gone. "Bye," I mumbled, shaking my head and feeling baffled as I opened the door and staggered up the rickety stairs.

This was her post-breakup modus operandi—she got my attention, then said nothing or shared a provocative word or two, and then ran. I didn't get why she bothered to interact at all since she dashed off and clearly did not want to talk. She could have easily walked past me on the street because I was looking up.

Slim did almost the same thing at the Obama election night party at the gay center. I was standing along a wall looking for a seat when she walked past me, tapping my arm for recognition (shades of the Elvis sighting), stood there silently, refused to say hello, and ran off when I tried to speak to her. This made me feel both dissed and frustrated.

The good part was that Slim's crazy behavior no longer upset me; it just puzzled me. These bizarre encounters made me glad we were no longer together. Was running into her synchronicity? Maybe I attracted her into my space so I could check out how oddly she acted. Or maybe it was just a coincidence. Whenever I walked around the East Village, I ran into people I knew. I was a community activist there in the 1980s and 1990s.

And I could not help but think of what Fiona, the psychic in Woodstock, had told me just earlier that week when I consulted her on the phone about 2010. Slim came up when Fiona saw all these sword cards, which she related to my past suffering, and warned me, "The fact the she can't even talk to you makes me realize she is moved by some weird energy. Don't ever allow her back into your life and don't be pulled into the past."

I would never do that. I could see clearly now. The blinders were off.

10

SPEED SHRINKING FOR LOVE:

FEBRUARY 2010

On Friday night of Valentine's weekend, I found myself on the exact same block where Slim and I saw a lesbian couples' counselor for several months in 1995. What a weird deja vu moment—to be thrown back here alone, not for therapy but for a "speed shrinking" book party tossed by my straight colleague, Susan Shapiro, who published a comic novel with the same title. The concept was modeled after speed dating, except you saw each therapist for three minutes. The quirky event had received lots of publicity and become superpopular. Since this one was being held near Valentine's Day, the panel of shrinks included experts in matters of the heart.

I planned to make the rounds of these love and relationship gurus. I was already in therapy, so this felt like cheating, but maybe this pressure-cooker environment could produce instant enlightenment from someone who didn't know my whole life story. If nothing else, I was supporting the event of a friend who'd helped me over the years.

As I approached the lobby, I practiced my pitch speech so I could get the words out fast: "Hi. I'm Kate. I was in a twenty-six-year relationship with another woman that ended badly a few years ago. I spent a lot of time reconstructing my life—everything is going well—and now I want to meet someone. I'm going out, but nothing's happening. I had a few first dates, but that's it. What do you suggest?"

I ran this through my head as I found my way to the main conference room of the Washington Square Institute, a big corner building with many small rooms for private sessions. I was early but knew from past experience these events filled up fast.

LOOKING FOR A KISS

The hall looked festive with sparkly white lights and tables filled with soda, water, wine, chocolates, and pastries. I sipped a glass of wine and chatted with my former writing students, many of whom had also studied with my colleague Sue.

As the agents and editors sat down at tables on one side and the shrinks settled into the other side, I grabbed a seat opposite a therapist. Shapiro introduced the guests and the two timekeepers. I knew the drill. You sat in front of a therapist and got three minutes to talk; you moved to the next one at a signal. I didn't like the woman who screamed, "Move bitches." I thought that was crude. When the male timekeeper yelled, "Start shrinking," I was ready.

Shrink #1 was an attractive woman in a red power suit. She was billed as a relationship expert who specialized in sex therapy. I raised the possibility that I was too critical when I went out and dismissed people for superficial reasons.

"What are you afraid of?" she asked. "Maybe you are not allowing yourself to see the positive qualities because you are defending yourself against possible rejection."

That line made sense, and if I kept judging women based upon their appearances, I might not get to see any positive qualities. Maybe that person dressed blandly was smart with a great sense of humor. I'd never discover that if I didn't talk more to her. This session reinforced the idea that I had to be more open, get beyond surfaces. I was taking this in and had another question, but the timekeeper shouted for us to move. That was frustrating, but I knew it was necessary to respect the rules.

Shrink #2 was a relationship advice columnist for Nerve.com, a popular website. She looked younger than most of the other shrinks, maybe in her thirties.

"Ask your close friends for feedback about how you present yourself when you go out," she advised.

So far, the only feedback I'd received via a friend was that this cute woman I dined with was afraid to date a writer. Since Shrink #2 was also a writer, we discussed how she handled that. She said she told guys that she never wrote about them unless she asked first. But what if they said no? I'd already decided I wouldn't date anyone unless I could write about her or us. This was part of my identity as a personal essayist, and I could write almost anything about me and Slim when we were together. Was my criteria limiting me now? I mentioned what my shrink said about my having "a guard rail around my heart."

"Who doesn't?" the speed shrink snapped back. "If everybody waited until they didn't have any baggage, no one would date. There is no perfect time to start."

She was encouraging and spunky and I could see why readers enjoyed her.

Shrink #3 was the only openly gay person on the panel; he was late middle-aged with a pleasant face. I liked that he helped people with coming out issues. He was a friend of a friend and I knew a little about him from reading her memoir where he was a character.

"You know my partner died," he reminded me. "When you've been hurt and then you go out, part of you is there and part of you is not."

I knew exactly what he meant, but I'd made progress healing that wound and felt whole now. I didn't tell him that I thought betrayal was more painful than death. We talked about the mourning process and keeping a positive attitude.

"When I go to an event," he continued, "I say to myself, *maybe I can meet my next lover.*"

I liked the gay male therapist and wanted him to meet someone nice.

Shrink #4 was a petite woman with offices in Los Angeles and New York. She was a relationship counselor and professor of human sexuality. She exuded empathy.

"It's hard to get back out there," she said. "I hope you congratulate yourself for doing that."

I told her what my therapist said about me being afraid to open my heart because I was enjoying my independence and was afraid to lose it, as I'd done before in my long-term relationship.

"It's possible to be independent and open up your heart," said Shrink #4.

I was working on this in my fifty-minute sessions but it was nice to hear it from another source. 'You are doing all the right stuff," she reassured me.

Shrink #5 was a Jungian psychotherapist and an astrologer with a magazine column. She looked more bohemian than the other panelists. I told her I'd seen another Jungian astrologer, who'd read both our charts after the breakup and said we had this horrible Pluto-Venus thing that only occurs every 240 years, and the relationship could not survive this messy configuration.

"Yes, Pluto may have caused resistance," she agreed. "But this weekend is a new moon, so make a list of your intentions."

Shrink #6 was the only one I did not like, probably because he immediately asked me, "So have you been dating any men?"

"Huh?" I said. "I told you I was with another woman all those years."

"I'm sorry," he said. "I didn't hear you." He looked like a metrosexual, one of those straight men who comes across as gay.

I let it slide because the room was very noisy. I looked at his card. He was a psychologist and wrote for the website of a popular self-help magazine.

"Are you depressed?" he shouted at me.

"No, I'm not depressed," I shouted back.

"Then unguard your heart," he ordered as I spilled my story. "Try a strategy involving numbers."

I gathered he was telling me to go out more frequently, but I had shut down to his advice because his style seemed so aggressive.

Shrink #7 was a medical doctor and an Indian. He reminded me of Deepak Chopra. "What do you enjoy doing?" he asked. "Stay in touch with stuff you are passionate about."

I told him I was into yoga and chanting and taking workshops related to spirituality.

"Go to places like Omega. Direct your energies."

"I love Omega," I said, suddenly seeing it as a place to meet like-minded women.

"But when you go there, are you always looking? If you project that too much, it might be off-putting."

I liked this doctor's approach and totally agreed with him.

That was it. Twenty minutes and I was speed shrunk. I've had over twenty-five years of psychotherapy, and yet I was surprised to come away from this experience with renewed hope, feeling positive that I'm on the right path. I was recharged and ready to amp up my dating energy.

I went to a women's dance run by SAGE, a group for gays over fifty, and a good place to meet fellow baby boomers. I feared the music would be dated, not the current indie bands I liked, but I took the subway to Times Square and found the club. I went upstairs, paid the fee, got my hand stamped, and checked my coat. As usual, I found my neighbor Janey with a few friends. I even ran into the shrink who was afraid to date a writer. Or maybe it was me and that was her excuse. I smiled and said hello and she said, "Hi, you look great."

I did look good. My bangs were long, I was wearing tight Calvin Klein jeans, and I had ditched the eye glasses since the surgery. We chatted and I asked her to dance and we got down to Rick James. She was energetic and brought out my best moves. The next song was dreary, so I thanked her and went to the bar for an $8 beer. It was busy and took me about ten minutes to get served.

As I turned around with my cold brew, I scanned the floor and saw Slim once again accompanied by the vegetarian with the bad haircut. But this time I didn't have my beard, my make-believe date with the hot yoga gal.

I was upset although I had no desire to be with Slim. I was no longer in love with her. I didn't even like her anymore. What bothered me was that she was dating and I was not. Only in the insular lesbian world do I have to witness this. Even in New York City, we did not have as many options for socializing as straight single people.

I got a good look at Slim from a discreet area near the bar. To my surprise, she didn't appear that attractive to me anymore. She had aged badly and her nose was bigger than I recalled. Either she looked different or my perception had changed.

I was flustered and decided to leave. I was not happy with myself for doing that. Why the hell did I care if Slim saw I wasn't dating anyone?

When I told all this to Dr. R., she said, "It feels like a competition and you lost. You have made a lot of progress in every area except that one. The last thing you want is for her to have something you don't. You want her to be miserable."

"True, it's upsetting that she's ahead in the dating area," I said. "What's wrong with me?"

"You left the dance because you are still attached," said Dr. R. "The fact she is dating means she is not attached. There is a part of you that longs for the past and that's afraid to move on. Dating has not been a priority for you and that preserves the past. It's not over in your memory and I can see that in some of your writing."

"Do you think I'm living in the past?" I asked, shocked. I saw myself as a hip, forward-thinking Village dyke, up on the latest music and trends.

"To an extent," she said. "Everyone struggles with this—not just you."

"But I thought I had made so much progress."

"You have," Dr. R. said. "Don't make this black and white. Remember what I told you, that your life is much better now than when you were together. You have a lot more of yourself, but you have a ways to go."

"Why would I want to preserve the past?" I asked, furiously scribbling notes as I sat at my kitchen table, hands free because I was wearing a headset as we spoke on the phone.

"It's like living in a museum and being the curator," she said.

I thought that was a great analogy and it reminded me of my mother who spoke of my deceased father constantly. Now I saw her as the curator of the Francis C. Walter Museum. I'd often described the house in Paterson, New Jersey, where I grew up as a museum. I'd been raised in a three-family Victorian house, built in 1903, by my paternal grandparents. My father grew up there, and my mother still resides among my grandmother's antiques. My mother lives surrounded by memories and memorabilia, which makes her feel close to my father. Recently, she was forced to have the entire kitchen redone after using the same stove for over sixty years.

A framed portrait of my father, middle-aged and handsome, rests atop his childhood piano. When I was young, he gave me lessons on the same instrument. In the '40s and '50s, he played sax in a swing band, but as we kids came along, he phased out an artistic career in favor of teaching and job security. When I was in grammar school, we played the band's scratchy 78 records on my grandmother's crank-up Victrola.

While I agreed with Dr. R. that part of me was like my mother, her preserving my father made sense to me, but my clinging to the years with Slim did not, I argued. My mother had over fifty years of positive memories; their marriage ended sadly, not badly. She had status as the widow of a respected educator whose mourners packed a large church. I was dumped and left with nothing, not even the courtesy of a post-breakup meeting.

We talked about how my parents were totally devoted to each other and their marriage, and how dedication was a running theme in my family. My mother wanted her children committed to her and my parents wanted us all to be faithful to the Catholic Church. When Slim had described me as a devoted partner, I took it as a compliment.

"You were too devoted and did not have enough of yourself," Dr. R. said.

"I always thought devotion was good but I must have confused it with love and loyalty."

"And you confused love and loyalty with giving up your independence."

"How could I have been such an idiot?" I wondered.

"You have never had a relationship where you could be yourself and be with somebody—a relationship without being devoted."

We ended this session with Dr. R. saying, "This year, make it a priority to meet someone. If you go online you won't have to worry about running into Slim."

I agreed with that plan and I hung up the phone. We were working long-distance since Dr. R. no longer lived in the area. When I ended therapy with her years ago, she had an office on the Upper West Side. When Slim announced she wanted to breakup with me, I called Dr. R.'s old number and freaked out when it was disconnected and information had no further information. What if she had died or retired? Luckily, I found her on the Internet.

It did make made sense that Slim would be less attached than I. Supposedly, she broke up to "explore what was out there." Friends and family all thought that was reckless. But she told me she "did not want to die wondering." I gathered she wanted to have sex with a woman other than me. I thought that was her way of shifting responsibility outside herself for twenty-five years of a chronic low sex drive. She had trouble owning her feelings.

I was shocked that Dr. R. thought I was living in the past, and I wanted to stop being a museum curator. I loved and respected my parents, but did not want to emulate their ways. Both my siblings stayed married, sticking like glue to spouses with problems that some partners would have found intolerable.

I was curious what others thought about my leaving the dance. My best friend, Jessica, felt it was not realistic for me to stay and try to meet someone and there would be other opportunities. She added that she felt sorry for the woman Slim was dating. Jessica, a therapy veteran, thought my shrink was too direct and should make me figure stuff out for myself more.

"It's funny," I said. "She was never like that when I saw her all those years in person. She got like this since the breakup. Maybe she thinks I'm not progressing fast enough?"

Ironically, my friend Leah had just read my column about "Speed Shrinking" and emailed, "You have changed so much in your attitude that you absolutely will be drawing the right woman into your life. Slim is in the past and you are cleaned out with room for another person. The right woman will love you in part because you're a writer."

I shot back, "I hope you are right. My shrink thinks I'm stuck in the past."

Leah replied, "We all preserve some things in our head. You spent over two decades with Slim, so it seems like you took the normal amount of time to grieve and be angry."

This was why I loved my friends. They got me. But I needed to discuss the museum thing some more. I felt defensive and misunderstood in the next session with Dr. R.

"It is not accurate to say I haven't been working on this," I said. "I work on this daily, but not through traditional means. I work on attracting someone through spiritual methods: chanting, praying, journaling, listening to meditations. So in my view, I have focused on meeting someone. I'm disappointed this approach hasn't worked, but I haven't lost faith."

"I didn't realize you were still doing all that," Dr. R. said. "You're upset because you thought the work you were doing would give you control."

As my therapist analyzed, I recalled what a teacher had explained in a law of attraction workshop: you can control your thoughts, but not the outcome. Maybe I had not manifested anyone because my approach was too focused on having control.

"I agree it would be good to add online dating to the mix," I said. "I can apply the law of attraction to draw someone nice to my profile."

"You looked to Slim for safety and security," Dr. R. noted, picking up the thread from our last session. "She was like a compass and you saw the world through her."

"But I have been navigating pretty well on my own," I argued.

"In some ways you have been able to leave and navigate on your own better than ever in your whole life. But not in other ways," she said. "When you start meeting new people, this stuff will come up and you'll see how part of you wants to stay in the past."

"Sounds scary," I said.

"We'll deal with it," Dr. R. replied confidently. "Maybe being scared is what it will take."

I came away from the session thinking that if I looked at dating as a healing cure, I could trick myself, as if I was opening my chest for reparative surgery. But that image made me sad since my father never recovered from this operation. Of course, he had a massive cardiac arrest, whereas I needed to mend a broken heart.

11

PUTTING MYSELF OUT THERE:
MARCH 2010

The only people who'd hugged me since the breakup were family and friends. No one had caressed me except my massage therapist. I did not count adjustments from my yoga teachers. From the minute I came out, I had always enjoyed sex. This lack of intimacy had to change. I thought about what my therapist said about my not having made dating a priority. Was that really true?

I reviewed all my actions in this area during the past few years. No, I didn't just sit home chanting. I'd volunteered at gay events, which everyone said was a good way to meet like-minded people. I collected tickets at the queer film festival, staffed a booth at the LGBT expo in the Javits Center, stuffed gift bags for the GLAAD media awards. But those efforts didn't yield any results, except free swag. Had I forgotten how to flirt?

On the cultural front, I attended readings and lectures at the gay community center and heard the spiritual writer Andrew Harvey and the graphic novelist Alison Bechdel. I finally made it out to Brooklyn for a panel at the world famous Lesbian Herstory Archives, an entire Park Slope brownstone packed with books, magazines, letters, photos, and other memorabilia documenting lesbian life.

Since I was actually making a decent living (for the first time in ages), I could afford to attend some pricier fund-raisers, like Empire Pride's annual dance, "Women's Heat," and the Lambda Literary Awards ceremony (the queer version of the Pulitzers). I enjoyed a backyard a barbeque with exotic vegetarian dishes, a benefit for Astraea, a global lesbian foundation. I was not wealthy enough for the $500-a-plate events, but $100 was doable.

I attended the LGBT Center's garden party—a packed food-tasting event held every June on the pier. That's where I was dissed by Slim who spat out my name when I walked past and said hello. (Now I understood why dykes who split up moved to other cities.) Slim was easy to spot because she's tall. She was talking to someone as I glided by. I made a point of greeting her, knowing it would have seemed rude to ignore me. Why not needle Slim a bit? (Janey said I looked hot that night in my Capri pants and white shirt that set off my tan.)

So this had been my basic agenda—cultural events, fund-raisers, women's mixers—along with my spiritual repertoire. But I had to admit it had not worked. Even though I supported causes and received tax deductions, I still had not made out with anyone. I was getting frustrated, especially since everything else in my life was going well.

I'd been hibernating for the winter and now it was spring and time for a fresh approach. I signed up for a dating event at the Center. Hot off the heels of speed shrinking, I was pumped up and willing to try speed dating again.

I felt anxious before the event. I meditated, drank a glass of wine, took a bath, and got dressed. I put on tan jeans and my expensive new black loafers with zippers and patent leather stripes. I donned a tight black top with glittery silver-colored Indian embroidery around the V-neck (neo hippie shirt). I threw several strands of prayer beads around my wrist. The look I wanted was urban yogini or "metrospiritual." I added some gel to my hair and was playing with it when the phone rang.

"You go, girl," said my good friend Crissy when I told her where I was headed. She and her partner Marie were coming into the city from New Jersey the next day and wanted to meet for brunch. I was going to church for Palm Sunday and invited them to join me at Middle Collegiate Church. Or we could meet later. Crissy was an ex-nun (another recovering Catholic) and I knew she was interested in this radical church. I gave her the address and hung up.

I hadn't been out on Saturday night in ages. (That once was my date night with Slim. We'd eat dinner, dance around the apartment, and have sex.) The Center was mobbed with a zillion events, including a retro dance with disco music pumping from the main auditorium.

When I arrived at the room five minutes before the dating event, the organizer was still out in the hallway with a shopping cart filled with soft drinks and snacks. Not exactly an auspicious beginning but we finally got inside and she put on some music as everyone nervously checked out everyone else. This was the time when we needed alcohol; instead, we got name tags and were assigned to rows as we set up folding chairs into two circles, the chairs facing each other. One row stayed put while the other rotated at a time signal. At least no one yelled out, "Move bitches."

I enjoyed talking to this bodybuilder who taught gym and played guitar, but she lived upstate. Three women from Westchester had arrived together—behavior that recalled high school. One of them, a short, stocky woman, who worked for a non-profit, complimented both my shoes and my beads. She did yoga and greeted me, "Namaste." I liked her energy, but I was not attracted to her and she lived far away.

I only met one other woman from Manhattan, a tall, thin, attractive dancer whose company produced old musicals. She liked the classical concerts in Central Park. I'm into the rock and funk of Summerstage. But should musical tastes be that important?

My most interesting conversation was with a hip-looking woman who I guessed was twenty years younger than I. She was curious about how downtown had changed, and we got into discussing the East Village in the 80s. She was awed that I'd attended performances at the Wow Café in its early years.

"Actually, I covered that scene for *The Advocate*," I said. "I'm a writer."

"That is so cool," she said, impressed. "I was in high school then, but over the years, I saw a lot of those performers at Michigan, like the Five Lesbian Brothers and the group that does the fairy tales—what's their name?"

"Split Britches," I said. "Yeah, the Wow Café was an incubator for many actors who moved to bigger venues, even Broadway."

"Is it still open?" she asked. "I live in Seattle now. I'm here visiting. I grew up on the Upper West Side"

"It's still around, on East 4th Street. I just read something about a new show. Pick up *Time Out NY*. They have the best gay listings."

"Thanks. Is it free?"

"No, you have to buy it, but *GO* Magazine is free—that's our gay girl paper. You can grab a copy here at the Center," I said enjoying my role as tour guide.

I liked this woman and thought she was sultry, just my type (dark hair, dark eyes, chin-length haircut that framed a pretty face, nice figure, and boho clothes. In fact, this woman caught my eye the second she walked into the room.) Plus, she had a cool job—sign language interpreter. But she lived on the West Coast and was too young. The event was geared for women ages forty and up. She was one of the youngest and I was one of the oldest. My hair cutter, who gave me dating advice, told me I looked fifty-two and could date someone forty. Could I do that?

I also met two aspiring writers. One woman, who had grown up in Mali, was writing a memoir and had attended a bunch of workshops and retreats. She was a large femme with facial hair and interesting jewelry. She was shocked when I told her I'd finished a 200-page memoir a few years ago and could not sell it, and that I was working on another one with a different focus.

"What is your book about?" I asked.

"It's about my life," she said.

"Any particular time period?"

"No, it starts with when I was born and then—"

She seemed serious and dedicated to her project but had not published anything. So I suggested she try to sell part of her book as an essay to get exposure.

"Someone else told me that," she said. "Thanks for the tip."

"Keep writing," I said as the signal indicated I should move to the next chair.

Another one of the Westchester gals, who reminded me of my childhood friend's Italian grandmother, was enthused about a short story class she was taking at the local community college. Her main goal in life was to publish something, anything.

"How is the class? Are you getting any useful feedback?" I asked.

"Every week, we make copies of our work and hand it out and then we read them out loud," she explained.

"Yeah, I know how that process works," I said. "I'm a writing teacher."

'You are? Wow! Can I ask you a question? How do I copyright my story?"

"Don't worry about that now," I said, realizing she was a total neophyte.

"So have you published anything?" she asked.

"Yeah, essays and articles," I answered. "I've been doing this a long time."

"I hope we can talk more about this at the break," she said, as I quickly escaped.

I did not come here to work as a teacher; I wanted to meet someone sexy and creative.

Besides the group from Westchester, there was another cluster of women from the far reaches of Queens. (The only nabes I knew in Queens were nearby Astoria and Long Island City.) For some reason, I didn't get to meet all these women, but I chatted with one who worked for the city as a housing inspector and talked about rats and roaches. I switched the subject and discovered she enjoyed the gay beach at Riis Park.

"I've been there a few times," I said. "But I usually go to the Jersey Shore. Ever been to Asbury Park? It's a cool scene—a gay beach and nightlife, easy to get to from the city."

"Heard of it, but I never went there," she said. Of course it made sense she'd go to Riis Park if she lived way out in Queens and had a car.

Some women were shy and I had to pull information from them. I was good at getting quiet people to speak—a skill I acquired in the classroom—but this meant I was doing all the questioning and not getting to talk about myself.

This rotating on the chairs, in five-minute increments, went on for about an hour. Then we took a break for soft drinks, chips, and pretzels, and resumed with everyone in a circle answering short one-liners the organizer presented, such as, "If people could describe you with one adjective, what would it be?" I said, "Quirky."

"What's your favorite movie set in New York City?"

"Annie Hall," I said, realizing my instant reply was a nostalgic answer. When the popular film debuted in 1977, I was starting my lifelong love affair with Manhattan.

At the end of the night we were encouraged to ask anyone we clicked with for contact info. I didn't like this format—it was too loosely structured and put too much burden on the attendees. I liked the format better at the last speed-dating event I'd attended, where everyone had numbers on their name tags, and at the end of the evening we wrote down the numbers of the people we wanted to meet. The organizer called us the next day with the phones numbers of our picks.

But I wanted to prove to myself I could do this, so I exchanged cards with the bodybuilder and the dancer. I initiated this. No one rushed to ask for my information, so I had no real idea how they felt about me. After I got home, I realized I was not going to contact someone living upstate. Maybe I'd e-mail the dancer who lived uptown.

I should have gotten the number of the sign language interpreter who was into performance art. So what if she was younger and only visiting? Maybe she liked older women or had cool gay friends who lived here. Maybe her mother was a lesbian.

I walked home realizing I was a Manhattan chauvinist who didn't want to date working-class women from the outer boroughs, or people outside New York City. I was instantly turned off to anyone who said, "I could never live here," as I thought I could never live anywhere else.

How to refine my options? Where were the arts dykes? The intellectuals? The women over fifty who live in proximity?

The whole concept of lesbian dating was so fraught, it inspired Mo Brownsey's aptly titled *Is It a Date or Just Coffee: The Gay Girl's Guide to Dating, Sex and Romance*, which I read twice. At a previous singles event, I met Pamela, a cute singer-songwriter who'd just moved here and we clicked over our love of pop music. We exchanged numbers and met for lunch, and she invited me to hear her perform at an East Village club.

Even though her gig was late for a weeknight, I dragged myself out only to find Pamela was there with someone else. I was confused. Were they on a date? Two years later, I ran into Pamela and learned she'd met me and this other woman right around the same time and was weighing her options. As it turned out she moved in with this woman who was violent and Pamela's life became a nightmare. (She should have picked me.)

I'd also met Kara, a talented choreographer and saw her perform with her troupe. She too had just moved here and was hopping from sublet to sublet, trying to decide whether to stay or return to Boston. We had a date during gay pride week the previous year—the 40th anniversary of the riots at the Stonewall. Well, I think it was a date. We both bought tickets and Kara came from rehearsal to meet me at the historical Stonewall Inn for a night of performance art featuring the iconic Holly Hughes.

I'd gotten there first but the tables were filled. I was having a good time talking to some other professors and listening to a funny comedian riff about academia. Kara arrived and I introduced her to my new friends.

"What do you want to drink?" I asked as I had the bartender's attention.

"I'm broke," she said, "I can't afford a drink."

"Don't worry," I said. "I'll get it."

"White wine, thanks. What kind do they have?"

That's when I realized that I did not want to date starving artists, not at my age.

Trying to hook up with someone was hard enough without this added layer of confusion as to whether or not you were on a date. This was a typical scenario: I met an interesting woman at a social event through a friend; we danced and talked. I sensed there was chemistry. We exchanged cards and I called and invited her to dinner. She agreed and we made a reservation at a restaurant we both liked.

I thought we were on a date, but was she thinking that? The food was good. I felt relaxed. She was smart and cute. To make my intentions clear, when the check came, I took out my card, but she started taking out hers too, insisting upon paying fifty-fifty.

She could just be a feminist who wanted to pay for herself, I thought as we left. Or maybe we were just new friends, going to a favorite neighborhood restaurant. We lived in the same general neighborhood and walked south from Chelsea to the Village. As we got to my corner, I made another attempt to see if this was a date.

"That was fun. I had a good time," I said as I leaned over to kiss her good night.

She turned away; I grazed her cheek and felt embarrassed. The next day I got a lovely e-mail saying she enjoyed meeting me and liked our lively conversation but wanted to pursue this woman she'd just met on Match. She was being tactful and clear, which I appreciated. She obviously knew I thought we had a date, but did we?

I'd encountered this phenomenon several times since I was single. Did straight people have this problem? Maybe going online could clear this up. And it would get my therapist off my back.

I already knew what my shrink would say on Monday when I relayed my reaction to my latest experience.

"Go online. When are you doing your profile?"

"Don't I get credit for putting myself out there?" I'd protest.

"Of course, you get a check mark," she'd say.

Knowing this would be on her agenda, I started drafting something:

"Writer/professor who practices yoga and meditation, enjoys bike riding, swimming in the ocean, listening to world music, dancing, going to concerts and museums, and reading, reading, reading. Loves living in NYC.

"I'm currently writing a memoir and looking for an attractive, spirited woman to provide a happy ending—or at least supply an exciting new chapter.

"I'm serious but fun loving, with a wry sense of humor. Loyal, honest, open, and out of the closet. Seeking someone comfortable with her sexuality, smart, creative, playful, kind, open, honest, supportive, self-aware. Prefer someone on a spiritual path, a person of faith, or at least a seeker."

I decided to post it at the next new moon, an auspicious time for beginnings.

12

THE FORGIVENESS TEST:

APRIL 2010

Just as I was gearing up to go online, I got distracted by a health scare. Beth Israel Hospital called to say my mammogram results were inconclusive and I needed more tests. I got more worried when a letter arrived the next day recommending a spot compression and an ultrasound. Although I was finally enjoying my hard-won independence, the idea of facing a serious medical crisis without a mate was daunting. Who would pick me up if I had to endure some awful treatment? Who would hold my hand and comfort me?

A firm believer in the mind-body connection, I feared I'd made myself sick because I had been angry at my ex for years. But I realized my anger had dissipated. Now I started bargaining with God. If I did not have cancer, I would forgive my ex, whatever form it took. I felt this scare happened for a reason—to push me into releasing more.

I didn't want to die now. I wanted to live at least another twenty-five years, to form a new relationship with someone kind and generous. I had plans to retire from teaching, live part-time at the beach, and return to writing full-time. I longed to see my great nieces and nephews grow up and win scholarships to college. (The oldest was only twelve.) But mostly I wanted to maintain the good health I had been blessed with my entire life. To me, this meant I had to do some serious emotional shifting.

I'd been stuck in a quandary because I believed Slim did not deserve a pardon for her cold behavior. She had left me, cutting off all contact, and leaving me in a fragile economic position. As a New Age devotee, I was bombarded with messages to let go and kept reading about how doing so was a positive thing.

In *The Age of Miracles,* author Marianne Williamson described pardoning a man who hurt her as "a blessing." In *Expect a Miracle,* relationship guru Kathy Freston said forgiveness makes us more magnetic to new people. In *Happy for No Reason,* Marci Shimoff called it "Spring cleaning for the heart."

As a Catholic, I grew up with Jesus absolving the men who nailed him to the cross: "Father, forgive them for they know not what they do." Jesus famously advised his followers to "turn the other cheek" and to be merciful to the ungrateful and the wicked.

When I heard this message growing up, I thought only a saint could be that holy.

As a yoga student for more than a decade, I tried to live by the principles of ahimsa, or nonviolence. Forgiveness came under that heading. The teachings of Christ and all the enlightened yoga masters were similar on this issue: whether you believed in heaven or reincarnation, practicing this trait got you a better place in the next life.

I'd gone though the stages of mourning my breakup with Slim—denial, grief, depression, and acceptance. But I'd gotten stuck on anger. I'd move two steps forward but slip back a step. While I feared that being unforgiving made me a bad yogini and a bad Christian, I felt letting my ex off the hook was wrong because she didn't deserve this gift. The truth was that I lacked the generosity to do this anyway. But today's scribes said to do it for yourself; it did not mean you approved the offender's actions.

Despite what my faith, the swamis, and the New Age gurus taught, I could not see how absolving Slim would make me feel better. My therapist thought I saw exoneration as a way to be open to a new relationship, although she assured me I could retain the anger and still find love again. Yet, when we'd discussed this two years ago, way before the health scare, Dr. R. said, "Why would you forgive that callous woman? She tossed you aside like a used tissue."

This unresolved issue had simmered on the back burner until I was called for more tests. Now I tried to imagine what forgiveness would look like, but came up empty. I promised God that if I was okay, I would stop cursing out my ex. I had already tapered off and was trying to quit since I knew this kept me attached in a stupid, negative way.

LOOKING FOR A KISS

Naturally, I attempted to put my upcoming tests out of my mind until the actual day. I kept reminding myself that lots of women get called back and usually it is nothing. Just my luck, the newspaper that morning had a story about Martina Navratilova being diagnosed with breast cancer. The tennis great (and lesbian icon) was having a lumpectomy and radiation. If she could get through this, I could too. My exam was in the afternoon, so I left work early to go home and get ready. As I washed up and changed into comfortable jeans, I wondered when I'd get the results. Waiting made me anxious.

When I arrived at the medical center at Union Square, I looked at the form and saw that I was assigned to a different suite than the last visit. Was this more serious? After the receptionist called my name, I went into the examining section, threw on a frumpy dressing gown, and checked my clothes into a locker. Then I went into another waiting room and sat with four other woman similarly attired. Were they also nervous?

The table had old issues of *AARP* magazine, and the one I flipped through featured an article about the best ways to treat breast cancer. I put it down and prayed this was not an omen. First Martina, now this. I heard my name called and followed the technician into the examining room.

"How are you today?" the woman said chirpily. "I need you to sign this. Then slip the gown off your right shoulder and come over to the machine."

"I'm anxious," I said, "about having to come back for more x-rays."

She took three pictures and compressed my right breast so hard that I had a red welt in the area above my chest where the machine clamped down.

"You can go back into the waiting room now," she said, all business.

I picked up a magazine but could not concentrate. What if I'd made myself sick and died without kissing someone new? What an ultimate blow. About ten minutes passed and the technician returned.

"Ms. Walter," she called, and I stood up expecting to be led into another room for a sonogram. "We'll see you in a year. Everything is okay."

"I'm okay?" I said, dazed. "That's great news."

I removed my clothes from the locker and went into a dressing room and started jumping up and down, my fists pumping the air. "Yes, yes, yes. We're done. Go to hell, you fucking bitch," I said one last time and walked into the corridor feeling relieved and unburdened. I did not have cancer and I intended to keep my promise to let go.

So what if I had just tricked myself into releasing this negative energy? I did not miss the irony that thinking I might be sick had cured my sick thinking. A health scare that I blew up in my mind took me to a place I could not reach through prayer and guided meditation. It was not a sappy kind of absolution, but it still felt empowering.

As I walked towards the East Village, I knew I'd never really understand why she left. I comforted myself with the knowledge that I had loved with all my heart and thought of that line from W. H. Auden, a fellow gay writer who had resided on St. Marks Place where Slim and I lived for two decades: "If equal affections cannot be/Let the more loving one be me."

It was a beautiful April day, so I sat at Veselka's sidewalk café, ordered a veggie burger, and focused on all the good stuff I had attracted into my life.

Still in a Closet: May 2010. I told the doorman that I was going to the party in Jacqui's penthouse apartment and he said to go right up. As someone who'd lived in the East Village for over twenty years, and now rarely ventured below Second Avenue, I was surprised to find a new doorman-building below Avenue A, but even the Bowery was gentrified now.

My church was hosting a luncheon for people who had joined within the last five years. When I got to the top floor, a welcome sign on a door indicated where to go. I entered a long hallway with polished floors and threw my shoes onto the pile. Adriene, the assistant minister, expecting a baby this summer, greeted me with a hug. Before seminary school, she was a Rockette and a member of the Dance Theatre of Harlem, which made her a great fit for this artistic church. I took in the scene as Adriene led me to a table spread with sandwiches and salads. Jacqui was on the terrace chatting.

I introduced myself to Jacqui's husband, John, a retired minister I recognized from church. He was tidying up the counter in their large living room. They were an interracial couple, both married before, who embodied the congregation's message of racial harmony.

"Nice place," I said. "Thanks for having us."

John explained that the apartment belonged to the Collegiate Church and came as part of the job. "Great perk," I said, wondering who furnished what I now realized was the parsonage, not just a spacious East Village apartment.

I grabbed some food, grateful the platters had vegetarian sandwich wraps and joined a circle of people chatting, napkins and plates on laps. Adriene sat with us and I introduced myself to the group, mostly gay men. One told a story of how he almost joined a Baptist church uptown until the preacher railed from the pulpit against the sin of homosexuality. The members cheered in agreement; he never went back.

Jacqui came in from the balcony and gave me a hug. Today she was dressed casual in Capri pants and a cute scoop neck top. "Hey Kate. Did you meet everyone?" Jacqui asked as she sat with us. "How's the writing going?"

I mentioned I was working on a memoir and that Middle Collegiate would definitely be in it. I'd already published an essay about my going back to church and it was a big hit. Jacqui had thanked me at the time and my piece was linked to their site.

"I still haven't told my mother I joined Middle," I confessed, hoping I'd get some ideas here about how to broach the subject. While my mother knew I had left the Catholic church, I imagine she wished I would return. My joining a new congregation would dash any hopes.

"Tell her we have many members who were raised Catholic," Jacqui suggested.

I doubted that would matter to my mother, who'd recently received an award from the bishop for her lifelong activism in the Catholic church. As I sat there at the party, I recalled myself as a child practicing Christmas carols on the piano and playing "Away in a Manger," mainly because it had one of the easiest arrangements in the song book.

"That is such a Protestant hymn," my mother sniped as she walked into the room. As a historic result of "the troubles," there was no love lost between right-off-the-boat Irish Catholics and Protestants although my mother's lifelong best friend was Lutheran.

"I need to have that Catholic chat with Adriene," I said, having previously told her that I was curious how she reconciled her traditional Roman Catholic upbringing with now being an ordained Protestant minister. What was that like for her? Maybe she could help me figure out a way to come out of this other closet.

"Yes, let's have tea," Adriene replied. "Before I go on maternity leave this summer."

We continued talking as new people arrived and were introduced and some floated back to the balcony. I wanted to get some fresh air so I went outside. I was standing alone looking over the railing when Jacqui came out and said, "So how are you, Kate?"

"I'm fine," I said. "Everything in my life is going well, especially my work. But I'd like to meet someone. That is the missing piece," I added, feeling vulnerable and too embarrassed to admit I'd hoped to meet someone at church but had no luck.

"I know, I know," Jacqui nodded. I could sense her empathy as she looked into my eyes. This woman exuded warmth and compassion. I felt she was not only my spiritual advisor but like another therapist.

"You're very pretty," she added, as if she could not understand why I was still single. "And in time," she trailed off as someone came over and stood next to us.

"Keep me in your prayers," I said as Jacqui introduced me to another member.

"Do you know Rachel?" she asked as we shook hands.

Jacqui went back inside as Rachel and I started to talk. Rachel had joined the church a few year ago and was raving about Adriene's Bible study class. That got me thinking that I might have better luck meeting someone if I joined a small discussion group. I asked Rachel what she did for a living (social worker) and what was her religious background, not a question I would normally ask at a party.

"I'm Jewish," she said, which did not surprise me. I had guessed as much.

"So you're Jewish and belong to Middle Church. How does that work?" I asked genuinely curious. "Does that mean you now consider yourself Christian?"

"Oh, no, I'm Jewish," she explained, "but I consider Jesus Christ to be my rabbi."

"Yeah. I've heard Jacqui refer to Jesus as a rabbi," I said. While I grew up knowing the Last Supper was a Passover seder, I had never heard a Catholic priest describe Jesus as a rabbi.

This was what I loved about this ecumenical congregation. No matter what your background, you were welcome and could find ways to make things fit, as I'd done.

13

A SECOND DATE, AT LAST:
JUNE 2010

The next morning when I came back from church, my machine was flashing. It was a brunch invitation from Mariana, a Latina woman I'd had met the night before at another speed-dating event. This was more fun and better organized than the disaster a month earlier. We had a mutual match. Mariana seemed spiritual and had just gone to see the Dali Lama. She was a cute femme with a nice figure, about my age, and lived close.

I called her back, explained where I'd been, and that I'd love to get together soon.

"Where do you go to church?" she asked and when I told her, she replied, "Oh, that's a great place. I've been there."

The connection felt like serendipity. Did Jacqui's prayers work that fast?

Yet I wondered if she mainly selected me because we were in the same age bracket—until she told me, "You're funny. I like that."

And I liked that she picked up on that aspect of my personality right away.

For my first date with Mariana, we met at the annual block party on cobble-stoned Jane Street in the West Village. Afterwards we shopped together for half an hour—I bought CDs and she bought a glass candy dish and a vintage framed picture—we walked up Eighth Avenue to Chelsea. Then we went for brunch.

Mariana looked stylish in a cute summer dress with matching blue jacket. She had a great figure for someone who just turned sixty. She told me she swam three times week. I was glad I had dressed up. I was wearing tan linen pants, a printed blouse, and a straw hat.

The day was super hot for June, more like August, and I was grateful for the air conditioning as we entered a trendy diner. As we sat down and looked at the menu, her phone rang. She got off quickly, saying she was on a date and would call back later. That was good to hear since I was tired of the "are-we-or-aren't-we" on a date confusion.

As we ordered eggs, she asked me what I taught and when I mentioned remedial English classes at the community college, she told me she had to take remedial classes when she was in college. That made sense. She came here from Puerto Rico when she was sixteen not speaking any English. Her accent was charming and I was trying not to let her screwed up verb tenses irritate me. I reminded myself she was not a native speaker and she had a good vocabulary. I needed to be less judgmental about my date. I started to wonder if the fact I'd spent many years as a music critic made me critical in general. If so, I'd have to switch that off when meeting new people.

Never mind that on my dating prep list of "10 Things that Turn Me Off," the top two were cigarette smoking and bad grammar. I was the daughter of an English teacher and our speech was corrected at the dinner table, the same as our manners.

Mariana may have grown up on the island but she was a New Yorker. She was a master tailor with a glamorous career as a costume designer for Broadway; it was a good union job and she knew a lot of stars. We both shared an interest in New Age activities. She touched my arm a lot as we talked, and I found out she too had been in a long-term relationship that ended a few years ago. After we split the bill, she invited me to her nearby apartment to see her backyard garden. Was she coming on to me?

She lived in a long, dark railroad-style apartment that she had bought when her rental building went co-op. The living room had a fireplace with family pictures on the mantle and the kitchen had nice cabinets with glass windows. I checked out her daughter's wedding photos, a portrait of her mother, and sports shots of her grandson.

She offered me a joint and I took a toke, which I realized later was a mistake, as I climbed backwards down the fire escape to the garden she tended for the building. Mariana turned on the hose and started watering, playfully splashing me as we walked through the garden. She explained how she'd grown this hydrangea from that one.

"Here," she said picking off leaves and handing them to me, "this is lemon grass. Smell it. And this is mint." I sniffed them both.

"Now put this in your hair," she said, handing me a white blossom.

The garden tour had a bewitching quality and I felt turned on by the time we sat next to each other on a bench. Or maybe it was the drugs and the sun. Mariana switched on a three-foot-tall waterfall and we watched the water cascade over the stones.

"Did you design that?" I asked.

"The super and I collect all the rocks," she said. "We build the barbeque pit too."

"Really cool," I said. "Must be nice to hang out here in summer."

"Not many people come down," she said.

Her dog was barking in the apartment and I needed some water, so we climbed back up the ladder and through the open widow. As we walked the length of the apartment I noticed several altars loaded with statues—St. Martin, St. Joseph, the Virgin Mary, and a few I did not recognize. I asked about them.

"I'm into Santeria," she said, which was what I suspected.

"That scares me," I said since I associated this practice with voodoo.

"It's all how you use it," she replied. "Can be good or bad."

She stared directly at me as we sat at her kitchen table drinking bottled water, and I felt like she was reading me. Or maybe I was stoned. Mariana had already told that me she was psychic when we were in the garden.

"I want you to pray the Our Father 100 times a day for a week," she said, "that is good for you with your Catholic background. Call me up in a week and let me know how it works."

I had no idea why I was being told to do this or why I agreed.

"I have to go now," I said as I got up, feeling unnerved.

"Come here," Mariana said as she too rose. We hugged and she felt good. As I started to break away, she said "You are very tense."

She let me out and I walked down the stairs and waved to her on the landing. I felt good when I got home, like I could do this dating thing.

I thought about my date with Mariana. She was witchy and spooky and she scared me with the Santeria and the unsolicited advice about the Our Fathers. Plus, I wanted to date someone who got me as a writer and who used good grammar. I found her sexy but I was not sure whether she was worth pursuing.

"Why not?" said Dr. R. when I described Mariana. "You like witches, and she was trying to be helpful with the prayer advice. Let that go about the grammar. Forget about the Santa Maria—it's a cultural thing."

"Santeria," I corrected.

"Whatever it's called, you look for things to discount people so you won't like them. You're both artsy and spiritual, you both have gardens. She sounds promising. You're afraid because she is new and different and there is an attraction. Why is that so scary?"

I fumbled around trying to answer Dr. R.'s questions, but I totally agreed with her about my tendency to find things to dislike.

"You are afraid she has some kind of power over you and that scares you because of your unbalanced relationship with that shithead Slim. You are terrified you will lose yourself and be controlled by the other person so you find these things to hang your fears upon."

"That sounds right," I said, glad I had Dr. R. in my life to point all this out.

"She is just a person and has no power over you, but you are afraid to care for someone."

I hung up from the session convinced my therapist was right, so I called up Mariana to ask her out for a belated birthday dinner. She accepted. This was the first time I had made it to a second date with anyone since Slim. I felt proud of my accomplishment.

Since I'd already been to her home, I invited Mariana over first to see my place and the garden I tend outside my building. Mariana was crisp and nautical in a blue-and-white pinstriped dress, red sandals, white jacket, matching rain hat, and cute shell earrings.

"You look great," I said as we kissed hello in the doorway and she gave me a gift. Thanks," I said taking the small wrapped package from her hand.

LOOKING FOR A KISS

"What is the matter with this apartment?" She sniffed. "It is so gloomy."

"Well it is overcast today. I usually get a lot of light in here," I said defensively about my sunny loft studio with big windows and high ceilings.

"You have to do something to this place," she carried on. "Burn sage or get a paint job. The energy is gloomy."

Who asked her opinion? I did not hire her for a feng shui consultation. I knew my place needed a paint job but I was on the in-house list for a bigger space and did not want to be bothered fixing up my studio at this time. Now I was afraid this date would be a disaster.

"How do you like those paintings?" I asked about the two large abstract canvases in my living room as I explained how I got them when an elderly painter from my building went into a nursing home.

"Those paintings have old energy," she said about the art on my wall. "Is not good to have them because they were thrown away and no one want them."

I wondered how many other famous artists besides Van Gogh died with work no one wanted. After she finished dissing my home, we went into my kitchen and I opened her gift. It was the vintage picture she had bought at the block party. That was sweet; she knew I liked it. So I tried to forget her unwelcome comments but she would not stop.

As we exited through my lobby, she said, "This whole building has gloomy energy."

I had to admit she was right about that. Westbeth was in a 100-year-old industrial building that been converted into artists housing over four decades ago by the now famous architect Richard Meier. The hallways were long and dark and cavernous and I'd heard legends the building was haunted. During the 1970s, there was a wave of suicides in the building. The famous photographer, Diane Arbus, had overdosed in her bathtub and several unhappy painters jumped off the eleven-story roof into the courtyard, earning the building the nickname "Deathbeth."

We walked down the street to my garden, a large sidewalk box with a tree in the center, and I proudly displayed my colorful handiwork: the impatiens were bursting with splashes of purple, red, white.

"This is a pretty plant," Mariana said touching a pink and white dianthus, "and it comes up every year."

At least she did not think my garden was gloomy. We cut through my courtyard to Bank Street, walked up two blocks to Bleecker and made a right into what had become a stretch of high-end designer shops—Marc Jacobs, Ralph Lauren, Juicy Couture—that had wiped out the neighborhood haunts—the card shop, the pasta store, the laundromat, the bookstore. I'd written two op-eds for the local paper railing against this gentrification.

"Isn't that clever," Mariana said, looking into a window where a mannequin was wearing a lace tablecloth as a skirt. She was seeing with her designer's eyes.

My point of view was that of a neighborhood activist, a crusading columnist who hated Marc Jacobs. (He was the first to arrive and now had four stores here.) I tried to explain to her how I usually avoided this area because it infuriated me and that I'd written about the negative impact of the changes for local residents.

She shrugged and said, "That's progress. What are you gonna do?"

We turned left on West 10th Street. I was taking her to Café Condesa, a bistro that was popular with locals. Café Condesa had a small menu but a good wine selection; the food was always delicious, and the service friendly. We sat at a window table.

We each ordered glasses of wine as we perused the menu. I was still pissed about her labeling my apartment gloomy.

"Is so nice of you to take me here," Mariana said, as she glanced up. "What is the matter? You look upset."

"I'm upset about your saying my apartment is gloomy. I don't think it is."

"Your apartment is cute, very bohemian, but I picked up this energy as soon as I walked inside. I can't help it if I feel things. What can I do?"

Keep it to yourself, I thought.

Luckily, the food began to arrive and I resolved to enjoy my meal. Mariana was busy chatting about her upcoming vacation with her daughter and grandson. She talked a lot about herself and I was waiting for questions about me. I'd come armed with questions about her work. So I asked who taught her to sew, her mother? grandmother? She deflected by saying, "It's a gift."

As our salads arrived, I saw her staring at my hands.

"So, Kate, you bite your nails. Why you do that?"

I could not believe this was dinner-table conversation from someone I barely knew and was taking out on a date.

"Bad habit, I guess." I had tried to quit but had given up. I knew stubby nails were not attractive, but compared to other habits this seemed pretty minor.

"Doesn't it hurt?" she pried.

"Sometimes," I said, relieved when the waitress came and asked a question. "Can we change the subject? This topic makes me uncomfortable."

"Sure. Let's talk about writing. I want to write a book about my coming to New York. I was shocked moving from the country to the city and I did not speak the language."

"You mean like the immigrant-coming-to-America story."

"I'm not an immigrant," she said huffily. "I was always a citizen."

"I know that," I said. "It's just a figure of speech for a type of memoir. So have you written anything yet?"

"I have filled a few notebooks," she said. "I have others but I burn them."

"Why don't you type up your notes and see what you have?"

"I can't do that. I'm afraid I may lose something."

Wait a minute. She wanted to write a book and did not know how to do word processing—?

"Can I read some of your work?" she said, finally asking something appropriate.

"Sure, I have a website—you just go there and click onto—"

"I can't do that," she said.

As she spoke, I recalled a colleague who needed my assistance to go to a website to request an instructor's copy of a text. I thought he was a dinosaur. It was hard to believe there were still people in the workplace who were computer-illiterate.

I was relieved when our dinners arrived. She had the sea bass. I had asparagus ravioli. She gave me a bite of her fish. The food was delicious. At least something was going right.

I knew Mariana had been in a long-term relationship and figured anyone my age who had never been in one was suspect. I asked how long ago her twenty-four-year relationship ended. "A few years ago," she said. "But it was on and off most of the time."

"What do you mean?" I asked.

"Well it was very emotional. We lived together for three years then we split up and went back and forth for years. Break up, then get back. It was so crazy, we both said our relationship should be a novella."

This sounded unstable to me. While Slim and I did not live together for our entire twenty-six years, we never broke up until the end and never saw other people.

"Was she Latina too?" I asked.

"No, she was Irish and German."

Interesting. That was my background.

We finished our dinner and skipped dessert; I paid the bill as she thanked me and offered to take me out for a drink. "Want to go to RF Lounge?"

"Sure. What do you think of the name change to Real Friends?" I asked.

Formerly called Rubyfruit, after Rita Mae Brown's famous lesbian novel *Rubyfruit Jungle*, this old-school women's bar on Hudson Street had closed for renovations and reopened with a new owner and high-tech decor, an appeal to a younger crowd. The name change was part of its makeover, but older women still called it Rubyfruit.

"I didn't know RF meant real friends," she said. "How you find that out?"

"Uh, I'm on their e-mail list," I said.

The bar was on my way home, so I agreed, glad this night was winding down. The place was empty except for a few women in softball uniforms. The bartender was inattentive, considering the place was dead, but maybe that was why. When she finally saw us, I ordered another glass of white wine and Mariana ordered a vodka.

"So Kate," said Mariana, "I think we have come together for a reason. I have something to give you and you have knowledge to give me."

I had no idea what she was talking about.

"I want to come to your class at NYU and learn how to write. I want to sit in."

"No, you can't do that," I said, shocked at her nerviness. "My current class is overenrolled and the room is very small."

"Ask for another room," she said bossily.

"That won't work," I said, based upon years of experience. "No other rooms are available. Space is tight."

"You have to stop thinking so small," she said.

Now I felt like smacking this broad. Was this the only reason she liked me? So she could pick my brains about writing? I help people all the time, but only colleagues can audit my class. I probably should have said this in the first place but I was taken back by her inappropriate request.

"Hello ladies," said a voice behind us. "I have permission from the owner to be here. I'd like to read your palms for free, but a tip would be appreciated."

I turned around to see a tall thin black drag queen who wore long false eyelashes and a wig. She was dressed in black and had a white gardenia pinned to her blouse, reminding me of a cross between Billie Holiday and Josephine Baker.

"Sure, why not?" I said, grateful for a distraction. Mariana handed the reader her palm and she pulled out a tiny flashlight. Everything the queen told her was stuff she had mentioned at dinner—planning a big trip, problems with relatives. This seemed accurate and I could not wait until my turn.

I handed her my left palm, and she said, "You keep comparing everyone you meet with your ex. You've got to get out there and flirt more. You are ambivalent about meeting someone versus being single and independent. What's your name?"

"I'm Kate."

"Hi Kate, I'm Simone, and now I want you to promise me, Kate, that you will go out and flirt with at least two women this week."

"I'll try," I said, thinking this reading was dead on.

"Now you have a nice evening, ladies," she said.

"Thanks. That was very good," I said as I gave the queen two fives.

14

NEW GIRL IN CYBERTOWN:

JUNE 2010

After the fiasco with Mariana, I decided to try online dating. As a new girl in Cybertown, I was attracting interest. I had been online for two weeks, exchanging e-mails and setting up meetings with women. Since I had no idea how to do this, I was following the concepts in Leslie Oren's helpful book, *Fine, I'll Go Online! The Hollywood Publicist's Guide to Successful Internet Dating*. From this savvy expert, I learned how to craft my image, pitch myself, and, field incoming offers. I kept updating my profile until it felt just right. People even wrote me, "It is obvious you spent time on this."

The Hollywood publicist suggested exchanging three or four rounds of e-mails, talking briefly on the phone, then setting up a meeting for coffee or drinks. The book offered great advice, although I had to make minor adjustments since it was geared for heterosexuals. To me, it made sense to invest time up front. That way we'd know more about each other when we met, and if the phone conversation did not flow, why meet at all?

Some women who contacted me reacted to my e-mail request as if it were an onerous task, indicating they'd rather just meet in person. I did not get it. Then again, as a writer I loved e-mail and was at my computer all day. Sandra, an attorney who contacted me, wanted to meet right away. She bristled at my suggestion to exchange a few e-mails but she reluctantly agreed so I compromised and waived the requisite phone call. I had to loosen up more. I was relying on these rules because I was nervous and out of practice.

Sandra and I set up a date for drinks and agreed to meet in front of the legendary Stonewall Inn on Christopher Street. It was a hot summer night and I was tempted to wear shorts but thought that too casual, so I settled on tight jeans and a white blouse. As I looked through my closet, I decided it would be good to have some new clothes for dating. I still had a gift certificate from Macy's from my winter birthday, except I hated shopping so much.

I stood in front of the Stonewall sipping my bottled water, looking west, expecting Sandra to get off at Sheridan Square. But as I turned around, a short woman coming from the east walked up to me and said, "Are you Kate?" We shook hands, introduced ourselves. She wanted to sit outside, which did not appeal to me, since it was 90 degrees. But I was trying to be open and agreed. I'd already considered where we might go, nixing the women's bars as too loud for conversation—and none of them had outside tables.

"How about the Cornelia Street Café?" I said. "They have outdoor seating."

"Sounds good," she replied.

Sandra was wearing Capri pants, a striped shirt, and flip flops, and as we walked down West 4th St, I realized she was about five feet, three inches—not that short. I was five feet, six inches but never considered my height above average because I'd spent many years with a much taller partner. To my relief, the sidewalk seats were filled, so we went inside and grabbed a table near the bar. She ordered a rum and coke; I got a beer. I don't drink hard liquor.

As the bartender went to get our drinks, I wondered why I'd agreed to meet an attorney since I viewed myself as too much of a maverick to be with someone whose job was to uphold the law. What tipped the scales in Sandra's favor was that she played bass in a rock band. Our drinks arrived and we started filling in our backgrounds. She didn't come out until she was forty-three, even though she always knew she was a lesbian.

"What took you so long?" I asked.

"I was a good Catholic girl," she said.

"So was I," I shot back. "Did not stop me," although technically I'd already left the Church before I came out at twenty-five during the heyday of the sexual revolution in the '70s. Like me, Sandra had graduated from a Catholic women's college in the Northeast, but other than that, our early lives could not have been more different.

"I missed the '60s," she explained. It was hard to believe that her being just a year older could make that much of a difference, but it did.

While I spent the early 1970s living in a hippie house on a lake in New Jersey, having sex with men and women, taking drugs, and going to concerts at the Fillmore East, Sandra was a suburban housewife who married at twenty-two and quickly had a baby.

"Desperate housewives of Westchester," I joked when she told me this.

"I was more like your older sister," she said, "in that generation."

"How did you know I had an older sister?" I was thrown off because we had not discussed siblings.

"Oh, I forgot to tell you, I found your website and read most of your essays."

"What? How did you manage that?" I said, annoyed. "I never gave you my last name."

"Oh, it's easy," she said. "I had your first name and you told me where you teach so I put it together and found this video of you on the college website. You're talking about some writing award you won. So once I had your last name, bingo! You have a lot of stuff about yourself out there on Google."

Now I felt blindsided. This smartass lawyer had researched me as if she were preparing for a case. For many years I'd written about my life (way before blogging). There was a lot about me on the net but I never had to deal with it on a date until now. If we were already seeing each other, I'd welcome the interest in my work. But it felt unfair for her to do heavy research before we even met. It gave her the upper hand as she kept bringing up stuff.

"You were born in January," she continued, "and you're the middle child, older sister, younger brother. His name is John and—"

"You have a good memory," I said, still a bit shocked.

"So I've been told," she said. "Now I want to hear about Slim."

I did not think this was first-date material, and why should I go into the painful details with a stranger if she'd already read the pieces I'd written about my breakup? But I briefly sketched in the details, telling her the most disturbing part at this point is that after all those years together, Slim won't speak to me or have any contact.

"Then she's a jerk," Sandra said. "I'm friendly with all my exes."

Unlike me, Sandra had never lived with anyone, which seemed odd, considering lesbians are known for their nesting instincts, and her longest relationship was four years. I gathered she had put most of her energy into her career. Sandra told me that lately she'd been having sexual flings with women in their forties. I was intrigued and wanted to hear more. I'd like to get me some of that and started thinking of this cute gay woman from my church. We'd been chatting that morning on the sidewalk after the service. She was forty-four and very hot, like a darker Halle Berry.

I was impressed Sandra was having affairs with women twenty years younger. While she played volleyball and was in good shape, I wouldn't call her a knockout.

"Where do you meet these women?" I asked.

"Mostly at work," she replied. "But it has no future. Look, I'm sixty-two. They don't want anything permanent with me. When they're sixty, I'd be eighty, so I decided to go online and meet women my age."

"Wow," I said, not ever thinking a forty-year-old would give me a tumble.

"So did you really see a psychic and an astrologer about your breakup?" she asked, changing the subject and once again bringing up things I'd never told her. "Do you actually believe in that stuff?"

All her background knowledge was throwing me into a tailspin. It gave her an unfair advantage and I felt like she was putting me on the spot. I could see why she was a good lawyer, except we were not in a courtroom. Plus, it was obvious she thought that psychic stuff was bullshit. I felt like I was being mocked, which upset me.

"I don't write fiction," I said. "Whatever you read was true. Yes, I saw a psychic and an astrologer and still do occasionally. I believe certain people have gifts in those areas."

Sandra looked at me like I was crazy, and I was sure she'd think I was nuts if she knew I attended meetings of Six Sensory New York. I was working on developing my own intuition, which was signaling that there was not a match between us.

"Did you read my piece about joining a church?" I asked. This was one of my favorite pieces.

"I skipped that one," she said. "I'm not into religion. I left all that behind."

"I did too," I said, "but then I rediscovered it. That's what makes the essay interesting—it shows a big transformation."

While I didn't expect to go out with someone who shared my idiosyncratic belief system, I'd never want to be with someone so cynical. Good to know. I could already see how dating would help me figure out what really mattered.

"This place is a far cry from the Catholic Church," I said, describing a recent service where three members of the House of Ninja vogued on the altar in front of a rainbow flag.

"I'm getting buzzed," said Sandra as she quaffed her second drink. "I'm drinking on an empty stomach. Why didn't you want to meet for dinner?" She said, irritated. "By the time we leave here, we will have spent two hours."

I was following the Hollywood publicist's advice about not having dinner at the first meeting. Foolishly, I mentioned the book to the lawyer.

"So you are following the rules in some stupid book."

"Only the ones that make sense. Look, we could have left after the first drink," I said. "You suggested another round and I agreed because the conversation was flowing." But flowing was not the right word. It was more like being examined and questioned by someone who'd read my files. It was fascinating in a sick way.

Sandra kept asking me about stuff I'd never shared with her but I'd written about in personal essays. My site has lots of material and as her Q and A continued, I kept thinking what piece had that info about my siblings? Where did I publish that one about dropping my hair cutter? How many pieces talked about psychics? Which one mentioned Ocean Grove? When I told Sandra I was going there July 4th weekend, she said there was someone new on the site who mentioned Ocean Grove. Maybe I should look her up.

As I did my best to answer her questions, I realized what bothered me the most was that she never once said "Your writing is funny" or "You're a really good writer." But she was not reading my creative work as an art form, but as a means to obtain information she could use. This was new to me and in the future, I could be more prepared for this exposure, but hopefully, I would not meet anyone else so tactless.

The bill arrived and I offered to split it even though her drinks were more expensive than mine, but she took out her credit card and I gave her cash for my share. I did not understand why she didn't order food if she was hungry. We were in a restaurant.

I walked her to the West 4th Street subway stop, even though it was out of my way. The air was stifling and now the two beers hit me.

"Nice meeting you," I said and gave her a quick hug. A handshake seemed too formal for someone who knew so much about me so fast. "Maybe we should go out for dinner," I blurted out, not sure why I said this. I had no practice ending bad dates.

When I got home, my lower back was killing me on the left side. I was not sure if this was from sitting for too long on stupid high stools at stupid high tables, or because I felt like I had just gotten off the witness stand.

"I think you need to be careful with your baddar," Dr. R. said when I described my last two dates.

"Baddar? Never heard of that expression. Did you make that term up?"

"Yes, I did." Dr. R. said proudly. "I made it up right now, just for you. "Baddar" means you are looking for things to dislike. It's a defense mechanism that keeps you from getting close to anyone."

"So it's like gaydar where you're sniffing around to see if someone is gay, except now I'm sniffing around with my antennae up looking for bad things."

"That's right. You can be judgmental in your writing," said my therapist, "but it works against you in person. Baddar means you have mixed feelings about getting closer and having sex with someone new."

"I love the term baddar," I said, feeling special that my shrink had coined a phrase just for me. "It's brilliant and I will try to tone it down on my upcoming dates."

I had meetings lined up with a psychotherapist, a hair stylist, and a recently retired art director at a major magazine. When I spoke with her and learned the name of the publication, I recalled that Slim had met with her, but never got any work.

When Dr. R. heard this, she said, "I already like the one who didn't give Slim any assignments. Make sure you turn off the baddar when you meet her."

15

MORE ADVENTURES IN CYBERTOWN:
JUNE-JULY 2010

I was very interested in meeting with Nadiya, a hairstylist, who looked like a real beauty in her photos. We'd exchanged a few e-mails and spoken on the phone, following all the steps recommended by the Hollywood publicist. Her e-mails were witty, and she posed all the right questions about my writing. Like me, Nadiya was a music lover and concertgoer, and we chatted about artists we'd seen and those we missed.

To this day, I regret not going with my friends to see Janis Joplin at the Garden State Arts Center. The singer overdosed two months later. And I still can't remember why I gave away my ticket to see the Allman Brothers Band, not long before Duane Allman was killed in a motorcycle accident.

When Nadiya and I spoke on the phone, the conversation glided along, so I broke the publicist's fifteen-minute rule and stayed on for half an hour. Nadiya admitted she was fifty-six, not fifty-four as stated on her profile, and I recalled what Sandra had told me about everyone lying about their age. As I got more savvy, I realized she did that because people cut off their search at fifty-five. I started thinking I should have lied about my age and if I'd shaved off two years, I'd be under sixty and get more matches. Too late now.

Nadiya looked like an attractive femme, so I was surprised to hear her voice. It was several registers deeper than I'd imagined. She worked at a ritzy midtown salon but told me the reason she did not list her profession was because people thought stylists were dumb. She was a native New Yorker who'd studied acting at HB Studio. When she was younger, she had the same piano teacher as Laura Nyro. That impressed me.

We had a similar sense of humor and had fun dissing all the ridiculous photos on the dating site—the many blurry ones, the woman in formal wear at a wedding, the intellectual in her cap and gown. (Was she hiding a bad figure or boasting about her PhD?) I'd already made a silly list of the pictures that turned me off, such as the woman on a boat proudly holding a big fish.

"I hate when people post pictures with a trophy fish they just caught," Nadiya said before I even mentioned this.

"Yeah, what's up with that?" I said. "Are they channeling Ernest Hemingway?"

I really liked this woman and felt flattered when she told me. "I could tell from your head shot that you had an expensive haircut."

Of course, I'd chosen a picture taken on a great hair day, but it was good to know it was effective. Now I wondered what Nadiya would think when we met in person. I was concerned because her profile stated that she was a femme who liked being a woman; it said she was not into the butch-femme dynamic and she wanted to meet another femme. She'd also mentioned just having a pedicure. I'd never had one in my life and did not care for painted toenails.

I thought I fell in the middle of the spectrum, more androgynous, but I was definitely not a femme. I never wore skirts and rarely wore makeup, but I wasn't real butch either. No one looked at me and instantly sized me up as a dyke. If I had to pick, I'd say I was a soft butch. I had a feeling I might not be femme enough for Nadiya, but I did not get the femme-femme thing. Where was the sexual sizzle without that dynamic butch/femme tension?

I called Nadiya up on the afternoon of our appointed date to confirm a time and place for that evening. "Drinks or dinner?" I asked, willing to do dinner since I felt we had a rapport.

When she said dinner, I suggested Café Condesa, which was becoming my new date spot, and gave her the address in the West Village. We agreed that whoever got there first would go inside and snag a table, so when I got there before her, I picked a spot near the window. I told the waitress I was expecting someone and went into the ladies room. When I came out, Nadiya was at the table checking me out as I walked toward her.

As soon as I saw her, I suspected I would not be femme enough and I picked that up in her quick appraisal. Nadiya was very pretty—with a cute short cut, dark hair, dark eyes, great features. She reminded me of a younger Sophia Loren.

"You look like your pictures," I said, as we shook hands, "but better in person."

Nadia was wearing eyeliner and a delicate necklace strung with either diamonds or zircons. It matched her earrings. Her silver watch looked expensive, like a Cartier. I was wearing a funky Swatch watch I picked up at a flea market and several strands of prayer beads on my other wrist.

She was another middle-aged woman who'd never had a long term relationship but she described her last love affair, where she and this woman from California met midcountry in hotel rooms for hot sex. When they finally decided to move in together in New York, Nadiya discovered her girlfriend was abusive and had to call the police to get her out.

The Hollywood publicist and other authors said not to discuss exes or breakups on the first meeting but how was I supposed to respond when dates routinely asked, "So what about you? Why don't you have a girlfriend?"

Whenever I mentioned Slim, I made sure not to come across as bitter. Yes, I'd been hurt and betrayed and amputated, but I was fine now. That was the gist. A close friend told me to say it was good she broke up with me because I was so much better off without her. But I didn't go that far.

Nadiya was family oriented and I liked that. Her father had recently died and she was sad, especially since Father's Day had just passed. This made me recall how bereft I felt when my father died over ten years ago. I still missed him at times but I assured Nadiya it got better.

We were having an intelligent conversation and Nadiya was very attractive, yet I felt no chemistry between us. I gathered Nadiya wanted a high femme, which I'm not. Once again, I walked my date to the West 4th Street subway station. This time, we shook hands and she said, "Thanks for the company."

A few day later, I was meeting Jill, a psychologist into holistic healing. When we'd spoken on the phone, I told her I'd just had acupuncture for my back. She approved. From her pictures Jill looked attractive but butch, with her hair almost in a crew cut. Her face appeared too lined up for fifty-two, unless she'd done a lot of sun, so I wondered if she too had lied about her age.

She had an office in the Village and wanted to meet at 9:00 after her sessions had ended. It seemed late for a weeknight but since I did not have to get up the next morning, I agreed. We haggled about where to meet in between her office in the central Village and my place in the far West Village.

"How about the Cubbyhole?" I suggested, citing a popular women's bar centered between both locations. Since we were meeting at night after my writing workshop ended, I wanted to relax with a beer, but that did not appeal to her.

"I don't like bars," she said, nixing that and suggesting this funky health-food spot.

I knew the place well and got there at 8:55 on the appointed night, went inside, scanned the room, and saw no one who resembled Jill. So I went back outside to wait in the oppressive heat. When she did not show by 9:10, I called her cell, and she said she'd been inside for half an hour. I went back inside, phone still at my ear.

"I was giving you until 9:15," she said as we shook hands. "That's my rule. Then I call."

Whatever, we were both here now. I wasn't hungry, and the restaurant smelled bad on this muggy night. I would have preferred a drink but got an iced tea.

Jill was an athletic-looking yogini who was wearing more prayer beads than I. She had been to India and practiced vinyasa yoga. I told her about my long relationship with the Integral Yoga Institute. We talked about our summer plans. She used to rent at Cherry Grove, the lesbian beach community on Fire Island, but thought it was ruined (by gawkers and gay men) so now she went upstate. I hadn't been to Fire Island in decades and never liked it. I preferred the funkiness of Asbury Park, which a travel writer compared to the East Village in the 80s. No wonder it suited me. Like many New Yorkers, Jill had never been to the Jersey Shore, where I'd been vacationing my entire life.

This was my only date so far where the topic of exes did not come up, but the entire meeting felt perfunctory and Jill did most of the talking. She had been in advertising, which she hated, and left to go back to school to become a shrink. Her practice was mostly gay and lesbian and transgender. She claimed her background in advertising prepared her to do therapy. "Everyone in that field had a drinking or drug problem and so do many of my clients," she said.

I was into healthy eating and regular exercise but I also liked to indulge (within moderation). I had a hunch my hybrid lifestyle might be too impure for her; plus, that comment about the time showed a prickly personality. A prickly purist. Not fun. I was relieved when they announced the place was closing and kicked us out.

On the following Saturday of Gay Pride weekend, I met Megan, the retired art director, for brunch at Elephant Castle. She was a bit taller than I, brown hair, nice haircut, not butch or femme, kinda in the middle, like me. She looked better than her picture, which was a pleasant surprise. After we ordered eggs, I confessed that I knew who she was when we spoke on the phone because my ex had met her briefly to drop off her portfolio and then obsessed over the follow-up thank-you letter. I was relieved when Megan asked for Slim's professional name and did not recall her.

"I'm sorry I did not give her any work," she said.

"Don't be," I said.

Megan had grown up in the South and still had the trace of an accent. I was amazed it had lingered after decades in New York. She was trying to figure out what to do with the rest of her life and had been taking writing courses. The conversation moved naturally, and after we paid the bill, she asked if I wanted to take a walk. That was a good sign. I wasn't sure if I felt attracted to her; she had a scratchy voice, which irritated me, but then I recognized this as baddar and decided a scratchy voice could be sexy.

"Would you like to go to see *Stonewall Uprising*?" I asked referring to the documentary playing at the Film Forum. "We could catch the one o'clock show."

"Sounds good," she replied and I was glad I remembered she was a film buff.

We hopped on the subway and got there with time to spare. As we sat in the lobby waiting for the show to start, we continued filling in our stories. She too was Irish and had attended Catholic schools. I realized there was a lot more ground to cover when meeting new women at sixty as opposed to when I was thirty.

The movie covered fascinating queer history, conveyed by talking heads who were at the Stonewall Inn that fateful night in June 1969. But the production suffered from the fact that there was no moving footage. Not one frame of film exists of this momentous event, only a few still photos. The filmmakers relied heavily on recreations done in a grainy style.

We walked up Sixth Avenue back to the Village, where Megan also lived. We

LOOKING FOR A KISS

discussed the movie and our plans for the next day. I told her I might be marching with my church, if I had the energy.

"I'll look for you," she said.

I never missed the Gay Pride service at Middle Collegiate Church because Reverend Jacqui always delivered an inspiring sermon on this Sunday. I wore shorts, walking shoes, a straw hat, and a cool T-shirt designed for the occasion. The shirt was grey with a rainbow design on the front that incorporated a cross; on the back it said "Believe Out Loud" and had the church name and website. The gospel choir and the traditional choir sang together, led by a guest director, who was starring in a Broadway musical; his solos soared above the chorus.

Jacqui's preaching blew me away as she evoked the memory of Matthew Shepherd, Sakia Gunn, and others gay martyrs murdered simply for being themselves. She noted how their blood must not be shed in vain. Jacqui started on the altar with a prepared speech; then she tossed her manuscript aside, went into the center aisle, and spoke from her heart, "The lack of welcome for LGBTI people at many churches in this country is an abomination," she declared, tears now streaming down her cheeks. "We can't rest until every church welcomes all of God's people."

"Amen!" people shouted from the pews.

"And after this service ends we are going to take that message to the streets," she continued. "Are you marching with me?"

"Yes," I heard myself calling back along with others.

"Can you sing with me now?" Jacqui said and broke into a chorus of "We who believe in freedom cannot rest until it comes."

Now the whole church was rocking, singing a cappella to this song popularized by Sweet Honey in the Rock.

After the service ended I jumped on the subway with other church members, and we went to our assigned place on 38th Street to line up to join the march, already in progress. When it was our time, we stepped out onto Fifth Avenue. I was used to marching without Slim because once her photography career took off, she was always on assignment that day. When our group got to 36th Street, our float (carrying the gospel choir) merged with us and we all cheered. We were off and marched in high spirits all the way down to Christopher Street in the Village.

I could trace my queer evolution though the various groups I'd marched with over the decades. In the '70s, I stepped out with the feisty Lesbian Feminist Liberation. In the '80s, I marched a few times with Slim as part of the Gay Teachers' Association, the group where we met. In the '90s, I paraded with the Gay Writers group, and now I was with Middle Church.

That night I got an e-mail from Megan. "I saw you and you looked great and the whole contingent looked like they were having a good time."

I liked that she spotted me and thought I looked great. Since we were both going away the next weekend, which was July 4th, we agreed to talk after we got back. I was getting used to her voice and looking forward to seeing her again.

16

THE BITCH IS BACK:
JUNE-JULY 2010

About a week after I went onto the dating site, I looked at the profiles of all the women who had viewed mine. There were about forty at that point. I skipped those who lived outside New York City and those with bad photos. That left about twenty-five women. I read them all, even those few without pictures. I knew immediately that one of them was Slim.

I wondered if anyone else would think it bizarre that a self-identified photographer did not post a portrait. Who was she hiding from? But I did not need a visual image to recognize her—the height, hair and eye color, zodiac sign, interests, and favorite places, including Ocean Grove, all matched her.

As I read Slim's profile, I started cursing. How dare she lead off her blurb with "Looking for Lasting Love." What a crock from the woman who would not even go to one counseling session when ending our twenty-six-year relationship! My tenuous forgiveness, achieved after the cancer scare, went out the window as I continued reading. She described herself as honest and caring and compassionate and comfortable with herself.

Did that mean she had now accepted her limitations as a lesbian who could only have a great orgasm if she watched gay male porn while running a jackhammer vibrator while she locked herself in the bedroom alone? My being banished from the bedroom during this ritual was the last sexual straw in our final months together. Looking back, I was so in shock when she went from being sexually inhibited for decades to seeming like a porn-and-sex-toy addict that I had missed clues hinting this might not end well.

I certainly was no prude. I was the one who had bought the lesbian porn and introduced role playing and light S&M into our sex life, yet Slim's need to pursue these new activities alone was a deal breaker. I got bored fast with gay male porn the few times we watched it together, and that upset her. I offered to try again but she was adamant that everything had to be just right for her to climax. I was a distraction.

"You lying, perverted bitch!" I yelled at the computer, sounding crazy myself. But I was glad I was no longer with someone who preferred solo orgasms to partner sex. That seemed sad, but if she was comfortable, then good for fucking her. I had nothing against masturbation, but for me it was not the main event. At this point, I was convinced the real reason for the split was her inability to combine intimacy and sexuality, which she took out on me. When I was not angry, I felt sad for her.

Now I was glad I had a sentence in my profile where I wrote about being being comfortable with my sexuality and seeking the same. Slim had a line about being attracted to upbeat women and I wondered if that was a dig at me.

No doubt her goading was a legacy from her Brooklyn Jewish parents, who disliked each other and were always yelling when we came to visit. Slim and I once argued so loudly that the upstairs neighbor called the police.

As I read her profile, I pictured her sitting in her Aeron chair, composing her description at the giant Mac in our former bedroom, where we'd made love for over two decades. I always had a good time sexually with Slim but she needed to be cajoled into having fun. Whenever we finished, she'd say, "That was great. We should do this more often," but we never did. I was often begging for sex, which she'd dole out sparingly or withdraw if she was pissed over something.

I did not miss the irony that the main reason I hung in there and tried to make things work (aside from being in love) was that I didn't want to be single and looking for a new relationship in my fifties. Now we were both online viewing each other's profiles.

The fact Slim was on the Internet confirmed what Janey had told me recently—that Slim was no longer dating the vegetarian chick. Janey had run into Slim a few times alone during the past few months.

My back had been hurting me for two weeks and the pain was getting worse, not better. The acupuncture only provided temporary relief. Now I was itching on my stomach and back. I thought it was caused by using the heating pad in a heat wave.

One night I was in so much pain I could not sleep, and my back felt like it was on fire. The over-the-counter painkillers I'd been gobbling had no effect. I was in such distress, I started crying. Then I went into the bathroom and looked at my lower back and saw a rash—a line of pimples where I had pain. Oh my god, could this be shingles? I wondered.

The next morning I was in my doctor's office. He looked at the rash, asked a bunch of questions, told me he was 99 percent sure I had shingles, and wrote a prescription for an antiviral medication. I was to take this for a week and should feel relief within three days, but he told me shingles could last for two months. My doctor said I had caught it early, which was good, and complimented me on my self-diagnosis.

When I told him I was going the beach for few days, he cautioned me to use sun block, which I always did anyway.

"Where are you going?" Dr. Goldberg asked. "What beach?"

"Ocean Grove and Asbury Park," I said. "I stay in the Grove but walk into Asbury Park at night to socialize."

"Asbury Park," he repeated. "What memories. My parents met there, and I saw The Doors at Convention Hall."

"Wow, so did I, " I said, trying to picture Dr. Goldberg younger and with more hair. "Maybe we were at the same concert."

Dr. Goldberg was my primary care physician for two decades. I thought it was cool we both saw The Doors in the same venue, same summer, maybe even at the same time.

"The good thing about this prescription," he said, "is you can drink and take it."

When I went to the drug store, the pharmacist told me it was common to mistake shingles for a pulled muscle until the rash appeared. I was relieved I had a diagnosis and a prescription that would help me get better.

I was convinced that seeing Slim's profile had triggered the virus. Shingles occurred when the dormant chicken pox virus got activated and attacked a nerve. This happened when the immune system was run-down and when you were stressed out. It was more common in people over fifty. Then there was the bizarre fact that Slim got shingles when she was breaking up with me. This could not be a coincidence. It had to be some kind of sick synchronicity.

Of course, my shrink insisted that getting shingles at this time was just a coincidence and not related to dating or going online. My friend Jessica agreed and reminded me that when I first felt the pain: I'd just come off a stressful busy semester in my full-time job.

I'd taught an Intensive Writing class with a new curriculum I'd designed and had to submit a portfolio and a report on the project. Plus, I was sleep-deprived from the noisy construction on my block.

"Don't blame it on dating," my friend said. "You're doing great."

My rash was mild compared to the scary pictures I saw on the Internet. My shrink did not think it necessary to tell anyone I was meeting since it was not airborne and I was not having sex with anyone. I agreed. Shingles was not sexy. Here I was finally dating and trying to hook up, but now I had this painful ugly rash, an obstacle I certainly didn't need.

I was going to Café Condesa so often now, the waitress treated me like a regular. I was sitting outside when Megan arrived and we kissed hello. Tonight she was wearing orange lip gloss—maybe she was more femme than I thought—but the rest of her look was similar to the first date: jeans, crisp white shirt, and cute red sneakers.

Over good white wine and seafood, we discussed the upcoming humor writing workshop she was taking in Iowa the following weekend. I laughed more than on any date so far and was curious to read her work. Was she a funny writer? Megan did ask more about Slim and I doled out information sparingly.

"So you were married," she said.

"Emotionally but not legally," I said. "We were domestic partners in New York City, which is a joke; it's not comparable to marriage," I explained, switching the subject to something more pleasant. I gathered Megan had never lived with anyone and her longest relationship was a few years. Her ex owned a house in Ocean Grove, a weird coincidence.

My plan all along was to suggest a walk to Hudson River Park after dinner to watch the sunset, but by the time we finished, it was 8:30, too late, so we walked to the Magnolia Bakery on Bleecker Street because Megan wanted a cupcake. We hugged goodbye in front of the popular spot and I said, "Let's get together when you get back."

"Yeah, sounds good," she replied. "Pick out another great restaurant."

The next day I sent Megan an e-mail saying how I enjoyed hanging out with her and hoped we could go to the sunset concert in the park when she returned. She wrote back that she too enjoyed our evening and would like to go to the concert But then she wrote, "I'm trying to figure out what I'm doing online, and I'm not really sure. If that's okay with you, I'd love to get together again."

Now what did that mean? It sounded like she was ambivalent—not about me but about dating. I wrote back thanking her for the honesty, noting that sometimes a change of scenery can help people sort things out. I added that I thought we had a lot in common. I did not want to scare her off, but I did not want to waste my time either. She replied that she'd forgotten to tell me at dinner how much she liked my writing (she had visited my website), especially my essay about a childhood memory from the Jersey Shore. *Good move,* I thought, compliment me on what was most important to me. I felt optimistic. She was flirting with me, and I was looking forward to a third date.

I was dripping with sweat the following Sunday when I arrived at Middle Collegiate Church, glad to be in air-conditioned sanctuary. Reverend Jacqui was taking a sabbatical in August so I wanted to absorb as many of her uplifting sermons as possible in July. Her message was based upon the Our Father. "Our ability to forgive is a gift from God," she said earnestly. "Forgiveness makes our burdens light. Let's drop all that crap—I mean, stuff—and let it go."

This was not the first time I felt like Jacqui's sermon was addressed specifically to me. Jacqui was dazzling in a purple dress and a flowing white jacket and silver bangly jewelry; her hair was in corkscrew curls. She liked to use call and response in her preaching and had us repeating "Let it go, let it go."

It reminded me of what yogis call a rolling *om* chant, and as I joined the chorus, I could feel my resurgence of anger toward Slim slipping away. I felt much calmer after I left the service. I'd been doing well for months until seeing Slim's profile riled me up again.

Like my minister, my therapist was going on vacation and we were having our last session for a while. August in New York: two of my support team would be gone. Could I manage without a substitute?

I filled Dr. R. in on my recent dinner with Megan. I said I liked her but it was going slowly. My therapist said, "Slow can be good."

I recapped that I'd recently met six different women and—to my surprise—blurted out that my goal was to date at least ten women, no, make that twelve women this summer (unless I fell in love before then). My lucky number was twelve. My birthday was January 12th, and on that date in 2009, I was offered my current full-time position. I'd also won prizes using that number. So I was going for twelve and was halfway there.

I already had two more dates lined up at the end of the month and had decided I wanted my outings to be artistic. I was tired of going to dinner. I was meeting an art historian to see a show on the rooftop of the Met, and I was going to Summerstage to see the band St. Vincent with an editor and music fan who lived on Long Island with her daughter, a teenager who approved my choice: "that's a cool group."

I was explaining to Dr. R. that there seemed to be two different categories of single lesbians in my age bracket—those who had been in long-term relationships that had ended (like me) and those who had short-lived relationships and had never lived with anyone. (In my book, anything under five years was short.) Then again, my frame of reference probably came from growing up Catholic, where divorce was taboo.

I was trying to be positive but I had to wonder how someone got to be over fifty and never had a long-term relationship. Were they addicted to work? Did they have intimacy issues? On the other hand, I could argue I'd stayed with Slim for too long. But even then, I'd have to say the first decade was good. I'd also heard that some lesbians were leery about dating women in my category, fearing we'd return to our exes. No fucking way, I thought when I heard that one.

"This is all scary and exciting," I confided, "that I'm actually out there dating."

"You're in new territory," said my shrink. "And you are keeping an eye out for the baddar. Sounds great to me, very exciting that you feel more open than in the past."

"I feel like I'm verging on something," I said, "and don't want to fuck it up."

"You are closer to meeting someone than you've been in many years and with excitement comes fear. You're being more expansive and making yourself vulnerable," she continued. "As long as you go over the same territory, it keeps you safe. But you are doing this even though you're scared. It's gutsy that you're not letting fear hold you back. That's very menschy."

"Menschy?" I asked. I knew the Yiddish word *mensch* meant a good person, but I'd never heard it used as an adjective. Sometimes my shrink invented words. I thought it was a nice thing for my therapist to say in our last session before her summer break.

17

THE FORECAST: JULY-AUGUST 2010

Everything important in my life was on hiatus in August—no shrink, no minister, no writing group, no favorite yoga teachers, so I was taking a two-week break from dating to relax at the beach. As summer rolled on, I'd been online almost two months, and had met nine women, had two second dates and one third date. I needed to sit on the porch, catch an ocean breeze, and escape into mystery novels.

I realized that during my sojourn into cyberspace, my sights had lowered. I went from wanting a partner to wanting a girlfriend to wanting a sex date to wanting a make-out session, to wanting a soulful kiss. I was no longer scared of dating because by now I had less anxiety and lower expectations. I'd figured out it was a numbers game—and who knew what I'd find? I was glad I was able to do this, although dating was tiring.

Right before my vacation, my astrologer, Bob, was sitting at my kitchen table on a super hot summer day, my chart spread before him, as he sipped bottled water and talked very fast. I was taping the reading. My astrologer was a former shrink who believed astrology was the first psychotherapy. Bob interpreted my chart with specific advice and connections to my current goals, and he made house calls.

"You have Uranus crossing the midheaven," he said. "This only happens every eighty-four years. It is very dynamic and exciting, and you're at a great age for this to be occurring. The next two to fours years will be the time to show the world what Kate can do."

"Wow. That does sound exciting," I said.

"Uranus makes an aspect to Venus and this only happens every twenty-one years," he continued. "During the next nine months, it's a great time to go out and meet people."

"So it's a perfect time for me to be online and dating," I noted, filling him in on my recent activities and how I was in a much different place than when I'd seen him a year ago. Bob nodded in agreement but cautioned me not to be too critical when I went out, not to use judgment as a defense against intimacy (shades of my shrink).

"Uranus likes to find fault. Don't do that if you want to find a relationship," he warned and then he went to his next major point.

"Jupiter crosses the midheaven next January to February and this only happens every twelve years. It is a great time to sell a book or get an agent. Try to have something ready by then to take advantage of this lucky aspect."

"What a fantastic forecast," I said.

"This is your moment, Kate," said my astrologer. "I'm excited for you."

I sat there basking in the good fortune that lay ahead for me, but I also wanted to know about my immediate future. A few days earlier, I had called Bob and given him Megan's birthday since I had a third date lined up with her, but I thought she was ambivalent. And maybe I was too. Or was I using ambivalence to mask anxiety?

"Ah, yes, the double Libra," he said, pulling her chart out of his file. "This is not a relationship of seriousness, but it is engaging, witty, charming. She is very iffy and I doubt she is available to anyone. I don't think she's the most sexual kid on the block because she's a very Neptune person and they don't go there well."

That was good to know and pretty much what I had thought about her.

A few days after my reading, I had my third date with Megan. I met her at the arch in Washington Square Park, where we were going to see the Charles Mingus Orchestra. After a little hello kiss, we made our way to the concert area and found seats on the bleachers set up for the event. An artist from my church was sitting behind us and as I introduced him, he said I looked spiffy. I was wearing a green vintage surfer shirt.

The widow of the legendary musician, Sue Mingus, introduced the ten-piece band, who played their arrangements of Mingus compositions with solos on trumpet, sax, bass, and guitar. As I sat there listening to a wild riff from a bassoon, I recalled how I used to write about jazz (much harder to describe than rock or folk). I felt relieved I was not on assignment and could just enjoy this evening. During a brief intermission, Megan told me how much she liked the concert and thanked me for suggesting it.

"It's funny how I live a few blocks away and I've never been to this series."

"That's always the way," I said as we continued discussing where to take her relatives from the Midwest who were arriving and staying in her apartment.

"Of course they want to see the Statue of Liberty, take the boat there," she said.

"Ugh, so touristy. Why don't you take them to Governors Island—it's so cool. The ferry is free, and you have great view of the statue."

"And Ground Zero," she added.

"But there's nothing to see," I said, "until the memorial finally opens."

After the concert ended, Megan wanted to grab a beer. Sounded good to me. First we went to Rubyfruit, which was depressingly dead, and then we went to the Cubbyhole, packed with a birthday party. As an alternative to the women's bars, I suggested Dublin, a hip Irish pub on Hudson Street, near my place and popular with locals. Megan loved the fact the bartender had a brogue and we both ordered Stellas on draft.

We were still getting know each other and the conversation was engaging. As we drank our second round, I asked, "So did you figure out what you're doing online?"

"I decided I'm not good at this relationship stuff," she said, apparently a reference to an earlier conversation about her exes. "I don't do this well."

To back up that statement, Megan told me she had only met three people since she went on the site. As she continued explaining, it was exactly as the astrologer predicted. I was not upset, maybe because I had already digested his forecast. Once we got this out of the way—that she did not want to go further—we went back to an interesting chat about how we first came out. I did feel sisterly with her, just as the stargazer had implied. I wasn't sure if I felt disappointed or relieved. She was the first person I dated who seemed to have potential.

When we finally left the bar, after talking for about two hours, we were the only ones still there. We stepped outside and hugged and said good-night. Two days later, Megan e-mailed, hoping we could be friends. I agreed. She was smart and fun and lived in my neighborhood.

LOOKING FOR A KISS

Before I took off to Ocean Grove, I crammed in dates with three new people—a shrink, a lawyer, and an editor. It seemed like there were a disproportionate number of therapists in the lesbian community. Why was that? I put together the date with the psychotherapist quickly. We were e-mailing back and forth and realized we were both in and out of the city a lot in the summer. We were both around that evening and lived nearby. So why not?

Mandy suggested 9 P.M. at Café Vivaldi. I would have preferred earlier but she had to give her sick cat a shot. When I left my building, I did not realize it was turning into a stormy night. Since I had no umbrella, I raced down Christopher Street in the thunder and lightening, trying to get to the café before the imminent downpour. I got there early for the date but just in time to duck under the cafe's awning as the rain began.

Mandy arrived shortly after. She was cute and resembled Ellen (as she'd described herself), but she came across as more butch than I imagined from her photo. I also thought she was a size thinner in the picture. Baddar, baddar, baddar. We had not spoken on the phone and her accent was pure native New York. I later discovered she was Jewish, from Queens.

Live music was playing inside, so Cafe Vivaldi would not be a good place for a conversation; instead, we ran around the corner to the Cornelia Street Café and landed up at this horrible window table where the door kept slamming and jarring us every time the waiter went outside to the sidewalk café. People huddled to stay dry while eating in the rain. Were they smokers or diners who sat down before this cloudburst?

Mandy was the first person I met who admitted anxiety about an initial meeting. I liked her honesty. She asked me about my experiences online. I was a neophyte compared to her. Mandy had been off and on the site for ten years and had netted two short-lived relationships; one almost turned into wedding bells, but crashed after a year. Mandy had a positive attitude, which I thought was great. If I had those results, I'd be disappointed. Then again, what was I thinking? I was still trying to land a kiss or a make-out session.

It was impossible to relax with the door slamming, so we left as soon as the rain ended. Still, I got good vibes from her. She too was vegetarian and into New Age stuff. We exchanged a few follow-up e-mails. I was curious about her degree of outness to her clients, and she explained that she was a psychotherapist who was gay, not a gay psychotherapist. If her clients asked, she told them. That made sense. I was a writer who was gay, not a gay writer, but it was different because I was out in most of my essays. Mandy had started reading my pieces on my site. She liked them. A good sign. We talked about meeting for dinner after Labor Day when she closed up her summer house. Not a problem because I was going away a lot too.

My next date was with June, another attorney. We'd set this up ages ago because she had a corporate 9:00 to 6:00 schedule and no free time during the week. She was attracted to the part of my profile that mentioned spirituality. Was I familiar with centering prayer? I'd heard of it but did not understand it. June was an Episcopalian from the Midwest. She was interested in Reverend Jacqui and my relationship with Middle Church. When we spoke on the phone for half an hour, she seemed pleasant. She described her job writing up cases for a law firm, which I thought sounded tedious, but she liked it.

"I used to write poetry," she said "but now I don't have enough time. Seems like you have a lot of time for writing."

"I set up my life this way," I said. "That's my priority."

Since she had studied art before attending law school, I suggested we go to the Met on a Saturday to see the installation on the roof called Big Bambu. It looked cool in the photos in the local magazines. She liked my idea and was a member, so I could be her guest. We met in the lobby near the information booth, found each other easily, and took the elevator to the roof. My initial impression was that June was a plain jane or plain june. Baddar, baddar, baddar, I told myself.

When we got to the top, we wandered under and around these huge bamboo sticks intertwined together with colorful rope, forming a gorgeous thatched roof. The New York skyline lent a modern background contrast. I took pictures to show my niece, a fine arts major into installations. June wanted to check out this historic display of women's fashions, which was fun. I could not imagine how much time it took to sew all those sequins onto flapper dresses. Then we went to the museum cafeteria to chat.

June struck me as overly earnest. She had been involved with this wacky ultra–left wing cult-like political party. That made me wonder about her. No, it was not baddar. I also thought it odd she had absolutely no interest in knowing about her father or his family; her parents divorced when she was a little girl and she barely recalled him. She was smart enough to realize she had adopted her mother's attitude and anger.

"But you have his genes. Aren't you curious?" I asked. "And you must have other relatives on that side, grandparents, aunts, uncles—"

"No, I'm not curious," she said.

I simply could not fathom her lack of interest but maybe that was because my father was a big influence on me. June was a good listener when I discussed my family, and I was shocked to find myself telling a stranger the story of my father's death from a heart attack and our false hopes that surgery could save his life.

"At least we all had a chance to say goodbye in the hospital," I said.

While I ate an overpriced salad and she drank tea, we talked about past relationships, which seemed standard during first meetings. Her longest relationship was seven years but they lived in different cities and only saw each other on weekends. I gave her my synopsis of the Slim story, realizing that in retelling it, I emphasized different parts to different people.

At the end of our afternoon together, as we were walking toward the train to go downtown, June said, "Did you say your ex was a photojournalist?"

"Yeah, that's right."

"Is she very tall?" asked June, who was also tall.

"Yes," I nodded.

"I had a brief tea date with her in the spring," June said.

Oh my god. It was intense enough that Slim and I were both on the same dating site but this was too much. My heart was pounding, but I tried to act calm. I was dying to know June's impressions and what Slim had said about me. June had a good memory and told me that Slim had changed her real name to an abbreviated version of the one on her birth certificate. (Slim was a nickname we'd invented when I wrote about us in my Queer City column in the '90s.) Her new name was more androgynous. She still used her given name professionally, but she was someone else socially. This bizarre news added to my theory that she was trying to create a different personality. Maybe it was easier to lob a syllable off her name than go to therapy. What kind of person changes her first name in her fifties?

I was trying not to seem overly eager as I pumped June for more info. Slim's work at a prominent news outlet had dried up due to the recession. (I already knew that from googling.) Now she mostly took pictures for this local right-wing rag (the one she swore she'd never return to).

Naturally I was bursting to know what Slim said about past relationships. June said she mentioned having been in a long-term relationship and one short-lived relationship since then. All June remembered was that Slim had contacted her, then sent two pictures.

From my earlier cyberstalking of Slim's activities on the meet-up groups, I'd seen both photos—one where she's hiding under a hat and looks creepy and the other where she had wild hair, so spiky and punky it made June think twice about responding. All this information (about the name change and the different hairstyles) signaled that Slim was trying on new identities.

I decided not to follow up with June—maybe the deal breaker was that she did not like the ocean—but I was grateful for the information the universe was dropping into my lap about Slim. This confirmed there was nothing I could have done to salvage our long relationship.

My final date before my vacation was excellent. I had not spoken to Stella on the phone and set up this date by e-mail. My standards were relaxing as I became more comfortable with being online. It was a good idea to talk first but not necessary. What attracted me to Stella's profile was her interest in current music. Her taste was not the same as mine but I liked the fact she too was into new stuff. Too many people my age were stuck in the past. Since I planned to go to Summerstage to see St. Vincent (an artsy rock band headed by a female vocalist), I invited Stella to join me for this free concert in Central Park.

Stella met me at the entrance ramp; then we found a spot on the astro turf. We spread out the blanket I brought and chatted before the show started while we shared pizza and beer. I liked her story: she was best friends with her ex-husband, had a twenty-one-year-old daughter she'd raised with a former partner. Stella was the only person I'd met so far who'd been in a long-term live-in relationship with another woman. She was into Buddhism and had a degree in philosophy and freelanced as an editor from her home in Long Island. The only negative was that she did not live in the city—I knew that my baddar was activated and shut it off.

LOOKING FOR A KISS

I thought Stella was more attractive than her pictures. She had straight silver hair pulled back into a ponytail; she was a little shorter than I and had a nice figure. She liked my butterfly tattoo and I liked her lotus blossom, although I'd never get inked on my hand. The folkie first act came and went; then we talked some more. I liked the mix of chatting and listening. I liked taking off our shoes and bumping our legs against each other on the blanket.

The second act, Tune-Yards, had everyone on their feet and it was fun dancing next to Stella as we grooved to the Afro-reggae beat and wild vocals. After another break, the main act, St. Vincent, riveted the audience for over an hour. Singer Annie Clark was beautiful, with an ethereal voice that played off her band's clashing sounds.

"This group is so good," Stella said as we danced side by side. "Thanks for turning me on to them. I can't wait to download some of their songs."

"Yeah, they sound great but they're better live. I have their new album."

It was a phenomenally good show and perfect weather—a bit overcast and not too hot. The crowd was friendly and it was not jam-packed like other times.

We left the park in a good mood, walked to the subway, and agreed that a concert was a perfect date format, a balance of conversation and entertainment, whereas dinner could be too intense for a first meeting. Since we were hitting it off, we toyed with the idea of getting some food in the Village but Stella had an early day the next morning, so she got off at 34th Street and Penn Station and I continued to 14th Street.

I followed up with an e-mail that I'd had a good time and I'd love to give her a tour of the High Line, which Stella wanted to see. We could do that and have dinner. She wrote back that she also had a great time but did not mention meeting again. That disappointed me but I decided to let this go. Her Long Island location made me pause.

I'd met nine women and had three to go to hit my summer goal. I was amazed at how I'd gone from being anxious about dating to being almost blasé. Looking back, I realized two of my most troublesome dates occurred at the beginning of my summer spree. I was glad to get some bad dates out of the way, and I liked my idea of attending events and getting a culture fix.

As I packed for my trip, I kept rolling around what my astrologer had told me.

It was promising. "Uranus making an aspect with your Venus is one of the great things to experience, and you have that from now through next spring," he said. "It means you can meet somebody who becomes important, who can shake you up and bring you to life again romantically. Nothing is holding you back except yourself, so go for it."

18

THE RECKONING:

AUGUST 2010

I was apprehensive as I walked into the parish hall of St. Mark's Church for the memorial service because I knew Slim would be there. It was for Renee, an old friend of ours from the era when we all lived on St. Marks Place between Second and Third Avenues. Slim and I had started a block association in the late 80s when our busy block was out of control with drug dealing and illegal peddling. We wanted to take it back.

We met Renee at our first packed meeting. She was a pretty, light-skinned black woman, a Brooklyn native, around our age. She lived a few buildings down the street and remained a dedicated activist after others lost interest or got discouraged. Our group was forceful for several years, and Renee was always over at our apartment helping to fold newsletters and stuff envelopes in the years before the Internet. From her work with the block association, she got involved with other campaigns in the neighborhood, eventually getting a job with the new councilman we helped elect.

Renee left her East Village walk-up and moved to Queens after she fell in love with Colin. We were happy for her because she'd been single during the years we'd been close friends and neighbors. The four of us met for dinner a couple of times after she moved, but it was not the same with her living in another borough, and then Slim and I broke up. The first time I spoke to Renee after that, she was shocked.

"You guys were a role model to me when I was single," I recalled her saying. "Your relationship seemed so solid."

In our last conversation, about two years ago, Renee casually mentioned that her cancer had come back, but she then she dashed to the next topic, so I did not probe.

Right before I went to the beach for my vacation, I got an e-mail from Colin that Renee was in the hospital and he wanted everyone to visit because she did not have much time. Colin got my address from my editor because he is the advertising manager at the neighborhood paper where I'm a columnist. I was stunned and very upset and forwarded the message to Slim, knowing she'd want to know. This resulted in us exchanging a few e-mails about how we were both sad, probably more communication than we'd had in years. We each went to visit, but fortunately not at the same time.

The morning after I saw Renee, I sat on my couch meditating. Then I started praying that she would have a peaceful passage. I was saying Catholic prayers, like the Hail Mary, while thumbing my Hindu prayer beads. After I finished, I did a few things in my apartment and then I opened my e-mail to a message that she had just died a half hour ago, which would have been right around the time I was praying. I e-mailed Colin my condolences, and the next day I left for the beach. I kept checking my messages to make sure I was back in town for the services.

I walked into the familiar church hall and scanned the large room. In the back near the kitchen, caterers were setting up a buffet on long tables. In the center, chairs were arranged in rows and in the front was a large bouquet of white flowers, two giant collages with photos of Renee, a podium with a mike, and baby grand piano. People were settling in as I arrived and Slim was already seated. She turned and saw me and patted the empty chair next to her, indicating that I should join her. I went over and sat down, shocked at her offering. I had no idea what to expect but I felt the situation was safe.

"You're so tan," she said.

"Just got back from Ocean Grove yesterday," I said.

"Nice pants," she said, complementing my pink Gloria Vanderbilt jeans.

"I got them in the thrift shop in Manasquan this week. Went there with my writer friend from the Grove. She loves vintage and I was glad to turn her onto that place."

"Which I discovered," said Slim, eager to take the credit.

Slim then mentioned she'd been in Ocean Grove this summer too. She told me where she stayed and described an expensive room. (It was not in a place where we'd been together.) She then asked what guest house I went to these days.

"Should I tell you my new find? Reveal my trade secrets?" I joked. "I don't want you showing up there." I meant it but I broke down and told her anyway, slipping into an old dynamic. "Fantastic innkeepers, and a block from the beach."

People were still trickling into the hall as we put our programs on our seats and walked up front to view the photos of Renee.

"She was so beautiful," someone behind us said.

"Yeah, she was," Slim agreed.

The service was about to start and Renee's partner, Colin, who was the MC suggested everyone get a glass of wine or fresh brewed iced tea before the event began. We went to the table in the back and I got a glass of white wine; Slim took nothing and we resumed our seats. Colin told us this was a celebration and he wanted no crying. Anyone who cried would get a detention, he joked limply. The two-hour service was filled with live music and speakers—family, friends, neighbors—extolling Renee and her ability to communicate and bring different types of people together.

In between speakers, Slim and I actually chatted, filling each other in on our families; after all, we had been related for over two decades. I told her about my mother's knee replacement operations and how she was going strong. I told her about the babies two of my nieces had since we broke up. I told her about my nephew's drug problem that had divided the family, adding that my brother was an enabler. She said her nephew was fucked up too, but I forgot to ask which one. When I told her my sister-in-law had a bad stroke and had trouble walking, she seemed very concerned.

She acted like the old Slim, not like the woman who'd dissed me for the past four years. But I was anxious the entire time we were speaking. I feared the icy Slim would reemerge as the conversation continued. I had little idea who she was anymore.

Slim told me her youngest brother had moved to Israel—no surprise because he had become very Orthodox not long before we broke up. She'd visited her parents recently and I asked how they were doing. "They're the same," Slim said.

"Still fighting?" I asked, recalling holiday visits to their house. She nodded.

But the biggest shock, aside from our having a normal conversation, was when

Slim announced, "I'm not vegetarian anymore."

"What?" I gasped. "You were so into it." Slim was the one who suggested we go vegetarian when we moved in together thirty years ago. She poured over books at the beginning to make sure we got enough protein. She became a gourmet vegetarian cook and eventually she went vegan, which I never did. Now she ate beef! This was bigger than a name change.

"I became anemic," she explained. "When my period was ending, I was bleeding a lot and the doctor told me I had to eat meat."

"What doctor?" I asked reflexively, since we shared many of the same physicians.

She refused to answer; her stony wall of silence went up over a mundane question. Now I realized her being anemic was probably the reason why she looked so haggard after the break-up. Friends who ran into her kept reporting back that she did not look well.

"When did you stop being vegetarian?" I asked, trying to understand the timeline.

Slim shrugged, that familiar shrug, meaning she was done talking. So that was basically it—a little family recap and the bombshell about her diet and then we sat quietly listening to speeches. Renee's adult nieces were around the same age Renee had been when we met over twenty years ago. The facial resemblance was chilling.

Renee's new neighbors in Queens described how she worked to establish the Sunnyside Gardens Historic District. That was just like Renee, I thought, remembering how we had worked to bring the Business Improvement District to our block. I knew many of the politically active East Villagers who spoke but did not recall the police officer who praised her, saying, "She was one of the ladies who helped to clean up this neighborhood."

At some point during this string of tributes and remembrances, Renee's good friend, who was co-running the service, came over and asked if we wanted to speak about her involvement with the block association. Slim shook her head no. I realized this was an important chapter of Renee's life that was missing, and I owed this to my old pal.

"I think I should say something, don't you?" I asked and Slim nodded in agreement. "Do you have a pen I could borrow? I didn't bring anything like that."

Slim reached into her bag and handed me a pen and I quickly sketched out a speech on the back of the program. Then I walked to the front of the room, stood to the side as directed, until Colin saw me and invited me to the podium.

I'm an experienced public speaker and my ten minutes went over well. I got laughs in the right places and tried to supply specific details other speakers had omitted. My voice cracked at the end, but I remembered Colin's rule about no crying. As I walked back to my seat, Slim and everyone else were applauding and when I sat back down she leaned over and said, "That was very good."

"Thanks," I said as I composed myself.

The service was winding down as a saxophonist played a soulful version of "Amazing Grace." Colin told us we would close with a recording of Renee's favorite song from *Hair*. She loved that play. As the music to "Let the Sun Shine In " pumped though the speakers, everyone got up and started mingling. The tears we'd been holding back started flowing. Slim was crying a lot, even more than I was. I stood next to her and said in a shaky voice, "If anyone could bring us together to have a civilized conversation after all these years, it would be Renee."

Slim turned to me, sobbing, and hugged me for about ten seconds. She smelled good.

"Are you going to stay and have something to eat?" I asked, still reeling from the unexpected hug.

"Nah, you know how picky I am about food," she said.

"Well, then goodbye," I said as she walked away.

That night when I got home I cried a lot over so much loss. Renee was gone, my relationship with Slim was gone, that period of our lives was gone. I got a triple mortality hit at one event. Slim must have felt the loss too and allowed herself to be close, if only for this brief time. The encounter made me think about what Dr. R. had warned me earlier: "You might have some longing or a wish that you could be friends, but you are right in that she does not deserve your friendship."

When I e-mailed Colin about this miraculous surprise—Slim treating me as a real person, after years of shunning me—he replied, "The magic of Renee was working."

My good friends were shocked when I told them. They described Slim's behavior as "amazing." One even suggested that someday I'd get an explanation. I certainly was not holding my breath. The morning after the service we were both back on the dating site at the same time.

Not long after the memorial, I went to Rubyfruit for a women's mixer sponsored by Out Professionals. The club has two floors, and since downstairs was less crowded, I went to that area to get a beer. As I walked to the bar, I bumped into a woman from my workplace who said she'd seen me on campus.

"I thought you were one of us," she said as she introduced herself. "I saw you in the library this week."

We then proceeded to list other faculty members we knew who were gay or lesbian. I was lucky that I shared my office with a professor who was a gay male and a writer. Our conversations ranged from puzzling over the sex lives of transmen to how our books were coming along. After I finished chatting with my colleague, I went upstairs and found my neighbor Janey, who said she'd be there. I scanned the room, glad that Slim was not.

Upstairs was more crowded, and my eyes caught the vegetarian girl who Slim had dated after dumping me. I was hungry and decided to grab a slice at the new organic pizza place down the block. When I asked if anyone cared to join me, Janey agreed, but I wanted to spin around the club one more time. "Meet you outside in ten minutes."

As I left this group and started to cruise the scene, Anika, the woman Slim had dated, came up to me. "Can I talk to you?" she asked. "Some place quiet?"

"Why don't we go outside?" I said, totally curious.

We knew each other slightly from another social group I joined after the breakup. Turns out Anika wanted to apologize for not saying hello to me the night last fall when I first saw her slow dancing with Slim. She had no idea of my connection to Slim until that night when Slim said her ex was there and pointed me out.

"I really felt bad I did not say hello to you," she said.

"That's okay." I said, thinking this woman was sensitive and more attractive than I'd thought. Even her haircut looked better. "It was totally understandable under the circumstances since my ex basically cut me off. It would have been awkward."

"I'm glad I ran into you tonight," she said.

"So what happened with you two?" I asked, feeling bold.

"I broke it off," she said. "She was nice, but I just didn't have the feelings you're supposed to have when you're dating someone. But she was not crazy or abusive, like some other people I dated."

Wait until you get to know her better, I thought. Anika was aware that Slim had totally chopped me off and I gathered she did not approve. She also said she sensed Slim had cut herself off from her feelings. I totally agreed.

"What did she say about me?" I said, seizing this opportunity.

"She said you were sweet and a good person."

That was the right thing to say but it did not mitigate the fact Slim had been rude and cold for years. Maybe speaking well was her twisted attempt at balance.

Out of the corner of my eye, I saw Janey exit the bar and do a double take. I said goodbye to Anika and then Janey and I walked down Hudson Street to get some pizza.

"Now what the fuck was that about?" asked Janey. "I can't wait to hear this."

19

CHANTING OPENS UP MY HEART:
SEPTEMBER 2010

Summer was winding down and I still hadn't met anyone, which was disappointing. I'd had a great time at the beach—sunbathing and body surfing during the day, socializing at night with friends in boardwalk bars with ocean views. People kept telling me I looked relaxed, and I wondered how long I could maintain that state. I felt relieved that I was cool during my encounter with Slim, but I was back at my teaching job, which drained my emotional and intellectual energy. On Labor Day weekend, I took one last trip.

As the chartered coach zipped from Port Authority Bus Terminal to the Omega Institute in Rhinebeck, New York, I hoped to be transformed—to move to a new inner place—by the cumulative effect of chanting for three straight days in a beautiful environment. I was very excited as I headed upstate for "Ecstatic Chant: The Yoga of Voice." A colleague had met her husband at this annual event a few years ago. I wanted to meet someone too. If nothing, else, I'd return totally blissed out.

I had already seen many of the hip kirtan masters in concert, but this weekend was like the Woodstock of kirtan, one of the biggest gatherings in the country. Kirtan is call and response singing, the repetition of sacred mantras in Sanskrit that name the Hindu gods and goddesses. When in the presence of a master, I could get totally high without any drugs. Kirtan is like a Hindu version of a revival meeting, where people feel the spirit, start jumping up and down and waving their arms in the air. I loved it.

As a music fan and yogini who enjoys dancing, it was no surprise I'd gotten into kirtan. It blended my interests and raised my vibrations. I was impressed with how modern American musicians had put their stamp onto this ancient Indian art, melding East and West, old and new. Guitars, bass, horns, synthesizers blended with the traditional sounds of the harmonium, flutes, tablas. The contemporary chant singers had created a new form.

My musical taste had expanded since the breakup. In my MP3 player, the rock stars of kirtan—Jai Uttal, Deva Premal, and Wah!—competed with Mary J. Blige, Neko Case, and Bebel Gilberto. I could be walking through the park singing a funky chorus, "Work that, work that," and then segue into chanting, "Nama Shivaya, nama shivaya."

In the spiritual classic *Autobiography of a Yogi* by Paramahansa Yogananda, the author described the first time he introduced chanting to an American audience. He was giving a lecture at Carnegie Hall in 1926. An American devotee told him it would never go over in the West, but the yoga master had 3,000 people singing for an hour. As he wrote in his overblown formal prose: "Blasé no longer, dear New Yorkers! Your hearts had soared out in a simple paean of rejoicing."

As the bus pulled into the parking lot of Omega, I wondered what Yogananda would think of hip-hop kirtan with drum machines.

"Now is the time to manifest, to open up a space," declared Wah!, my favorite artist, who played the first night. *Yes*, I thought to myself. *That is why I'm here.*

If anyone held the title of sexy kirtan star, it was Wah! An attractive middle-aged woman with a slender curvy figure and long hair, she sang and played bass. I had seen Wah! several times, but this night her band included a guy on vocal percussion doing beat box. She always pushed the chanting envelope with her arrangements.

Wah! had dropped out of Oberlin College's music department to study in India, then returned to finish her degree. Critics compared her sultry singing and slinky jazzy sound to Sade. I found Wah!'s voice prettier, more ethereal, with a larger range. I adored her recent album, *Love Holding Love*, and felt happy and free rocking out to it in my apartment.

At Omega, I carved out a space to join those dancing, picking up new gestures from the women around me. A few sexy females had erotic moves, like belly dancing meets trance dancing. I held my own, even though I didn't wear the outfit popular with what I called the "yoga femmes"—harem pants with spaghetti-strap shirts or colorful skirts with gauzy scarves wrapped around the shoulders. I wore shorts all day and sweatpants at night, but I did have lots of beads around my wrist. The men sported bandanas on their heads or Rasta hats.

On Friday night, Wah! joined the opening singer, Snatam Kaur, who set the tone by telling us "You have nothing to do but chant all weekend and go crazy."

This was the first time I'd heard Snatam Kaur, a beautiful woman with a gorgeous voice who sings and plays the harmonium and violin and looks stunning and mystical in her bejeweled white turban. She and her virtuoso guitar player (a Grateful Dead fanatic with a long beard) are Sikhs who wear turbans and robes. They harmonized seamlessly, and their interplay was kicked up by a terrific Indian drummer.

I was blown away by the purity of Snatam's voice and saw her every time she appeared. Her performances were like a musical meditation. When she led us in a breathing exercise that released anger through our third eye, I felt calm and peaceful. When she asked the audience to hold hands, I could literally feel the energy going up and down my spine.

Snatam was raised in California by musical parents who were Sikhs and into devotional music and the teachings of Yogi Bhajan. She lived in India and was adopted by a chant master who taught her about the sound current. Something was flowing from her and it really got to me.

The second time I saw Snatam, I started crying as we sang over and over "I am a child of God. I am a child of God. I am a child of God…od, od, od." I felt so moved by the chanting and her angelic voice, tears came to my eyes. I also happened to be sitting next to a cute twenty-something lesbian couple who were holding hands, and I recalled myself at that age and wished I knew then what I know now about promises of love. Or maybe it was better I did not know?

That day at lunch I ran into Mary Ellen, a colleague from Six Sensory New York and told her I was crying during the concert. "Her voice is heart-opening," she said.

The third time I saw Snatam, her guitarist directed everyone to stand and put our hands on the shoulders of the persons next to us and to sway.

"Yes, this is the Kumbaya moment," he joked. I was glad these devotional singers also had a sense of humor.

LOOKING FOR A KISS

On my left was a woman about my height and on my right was a much taller man. It was a stretch to reach his shoulder. I had already talked to Karen, my neighbor to my left, while we were waiting for the concert to start. Karen had lost her voice over a year ago and was seeking various alternative treatments and came to the vocal festival to find a cure.

As we swayed in a long line, everyone singing "We are the people, the people of God. Let us people, love today," Karen looked me in the eye and smiled. Too bad she was straight. I liked touching and being touched. I had forgotten how good that felt.

I took a break from the chanting and decided to visit the Wellness Center and treat myself to a massage. But as I scanned the brochure, the offerings under soul work caught my eye. I set up a reading with Kia, an intuitive energy healer who practiced healing touch.

The Wellness Center was a rustic country cabin. After clients checked in at the desk, we waited outside on the porch in wicker chairs until the practitioner called our name. Kia came out to fetch me. She was a large Asian woman, about my age, dressed in a flowered muumuu. She had a pretty face and a hip haircut and cool glasses. She led me to a beautiful wood-paneled room where I lay on a massage table looking at the clouds through a skylight. It was an idyllic setting and the light in the space kept changing as the clouds moved.

As I settled onto the table, Kia asked me what needed healing. I told her about the traumatic breakup several years ago, and how I was trying to make the last steps in my recovery, how I wanted to open my heart to meet someone new. She picked up a crystal that was attached to a cord and waved it over my body, like a pendulum. Then she put that down and she held her hand about six inches above my body and moved it around. Similar to Reiki, I could feel the force of the energy moving in that space between us.

"She is coming," Kia said, her eyes closed. "I see you at Omega holding hands with her. She is coming within the next two to three months. This person likes the country. You will have two residences, and she will be intellectual, maybe literary, and will respect your need for solitude as a writer."

This sounded reassuring. and I could not wait to hear more as Kia continued moving her hand over my body, occasionally touching my sides.

"She is playful, younger, and may have some of the characteristics of your ex, but don't reject her for that. The old relationship was unbalanced."

"That's true," I said.

"But you are a balanced person, although I detect a little imbalance between the second and third chakras. Your old partner did not feel adequate. She had low self-esteem."

"That's interesting," I said. "This new person—do you get any sense where I will meet her or what type of career she has?"

"I'm picking up that she does work that involves getting assignments," Kia said.

"Oh. That sounds like my ex. She got assignments. Could you be picking her up?"

"Possibly. What type of work did she do?"

"Photojournalist."

"Then it's her," said Kia. "I was getting a photographer."

"Get her out. Get her out of my system," I said, feeling confident in this woman's abilities.

Kia closed her eyes again and waved her right hand over me and I could feel the force of the energy moving between us.

"That should help," she said and then paused, as if moving to a new topic. "Another thing I am getting is some kind of renovation to your living space. Does that make sense to you?" Kia asked.

"Well. I'm on a list to get a bigger apartment in my building," I said. "Maybe it's related to that? I've been waiting for years."

"Yes, I think it has to do with moving," Kia said. "It will be happening soon."

"All this sounds great," I said, "A new girlfriend, a new apartment."

"I wanted to ask you," said Kia. "Would you mind if I played matchmaker? I love doing that and I meet a lot of people in my work here. Can I contact you in the city?"

"Sure. That would be fine," I said, not that surprised because Kia had struck me as a yenta. "You have my info on the form I filled out."

The reading was winding down and Kia gave me a mantra to repeat everyday: "I am in balance in relationship, in love, peace, and harmony." Finally, she asked me my favorite color.

"It used to be blue but I'm going with lavender."

"This is for you," Kia said, placing a tiny heart-shaped lavender crystal into a plastic bag. "And this is for you to give to her," she said, adding a clear heart-shaped crystal to the pouch.

"Thank you," I said getting up from the table. As I left the Wellness Center and walked back to my cabin I felt different, lighter, like I had shifted emotional gears.

Later that afternoon, as I was coming back from the lake, I saw Kia strolling the grounds. She smiled at me and said, "The energy is really moving this weekend."

I knew that Saturday night would rock, and I was excited about seeing Jai Uttal. He sings and plays guitar and the harmonium and blew me away when I first saw him in the city. This night he was surrounded by a large ensemble: several drummers, backup singers, a violinist, bassist, and a flutist. I was psyched by the big group. Born in Brooklyn to Jewish parents, Uttal started out playing R&B and discovered Indian music in his teens.

Uttal sang "Rama, Rama, Bolo Ram," which everyone picked up, and then he took off, starting slowly, then getting faster and faster. I felt myself getting higher as I tried to keep up. Uttal and the drummers worked the audience into a frenzied state. The violinist added a jazzy edge and the flute lifted us above the percussion. This high energy pace went on for over an hour, everyone going crazy and collapsing when it ended. By now it was 1:00 A.M. and I decided to go to bed. I was not staying up chanting until dawn. When I left the hall, people were sitting around a bonfire on the lawn drinking chai served from a large urn.

The music started later on Sunday morning to give people a chance to sleep in, but I was up early. The grounds were quiet as people passed each other on the paths and whispered "Good morning" on their way to yoga class or breakfast in the dining hall. The silence was profound; only the birds and insects were making a racket. The pine-scented air was so restorative that just breathing it cleared my head. I walked the labyrinth and sat outside and took in all the energy of the place and prayed to the enlightened masters—Jesus, Buddha, Krishna—for guidance. I chanted as I walked along the roads lined with sayings written in colorful chalk: You are bliss. Feel the Spirit. Namaste.

After breakfast with amazing fresh yogurt from the local dairy farm, I visited the Baba Ram Das Library. Built in the shape of a lotus, the building contains over

7,000 volumes of spiritual and self-help books. I browsed the shelves and picked up *The Lost Years of Jesus*. I'd recently become fascinated by the concept that Jesus traveled to the East, mainly India and Nepal, and studied with Yogic masters for eighteen years.

This storyline appealed to me because it made it easier to meld my kookie mishmash of Christian-Hindu beliefs and embrace Jesus as my guru. I had worked hard to replace the belief system of my religious Catholic family with elements that spoke to me now.

At the final chant session, Shyamdas, a kirtan master and Sanskrit scholar who's lived in India the past forty years, told us, "This whole fricking thing is one bliss ball."

Shyamdas was joined on stage by Jai Uttal and others for a wild jam session with the singers trading lines. The audience surged forward for better views. Dressed in the orange colors of a swami, Shyamdas said wisely, "If you love yourself, you love the world."

On the ride back to New York City, a woman asked us if she could play a chant CD. It was a smooth way to transition to reality. I curled up into a ball—a bliss ball. I had opened up my heart through chanting. I had shut down the baddar through therapy. I had an intuitive healer remove the traces of my ex. As we zipped across the Tappan Zee Bridge and I looked down at the vast Hudson River, I felt a shift, like I was no longer that attached to the past. The energy was flowing and now I was ready to manifest.

20

NEW INTEREST:
SEPTEMBER 2010

I was adjusting to my busier fall schedule and trying to find time to fit in dating. Beside teaching and grading student papers and writing my column, I was producing a literary reading in Westbeth as part of an arts festival celebrating the complex's fortieth anniversary. Organizing this event was my way to give back to the community.

In the midst of this planning and publicizing, I heard from this woman who wanted to meet me. Chaz was a friend of my friend Paul, who was playing matchmaker. He had mentioned her when we recently had dinner together. Paul was a fifty-something, good-looking gay man, a former student I'd met years ago. Since Paul lived in New Jersey, and we didn't see each other often, he didn't know me that well. He didn't know Chaz well either. They'd met through a mutual lesbian friend. Paul said Chaz had also been dumped from a long-term relationship a few years ago and she was around my age.

"I like her," he said as we waited for our table and he filled me in. "She owns her own home. She keeps in shape and she seems really nice. She's a good cook too. I think you two should meet."

"But she's a cop," I protested. "And she lives in New Jersey. I'm an old hippie, a writer who lives in the Village. What would we have in common?"

"Look, I've already told her about you and she is interested."

"What? You did?" I said, startled.

"Yeah, and I'd like to give her your e-mail."

"Alright, alright," I said, to get Paul to stop. I also remembered what my astrologer said about meeting as many people as possible and what my shrink said about baddar. And I flashed back to the tarot reading I had with Lexa in late July.

Lexa was expensive so I was only seeing her for half an hour and having two layouts—one about my writing career and one about relationships. I'd been cutting back on readings and hadn't been to her East Village apartment in a year. I filled her in about my new book project and asked for feedback as I shuffled the cards and cut the deck three times. She spread the cards out and started to interpret.

"This looks great," she said. "The ace of clubs is the outcome and you have three aces. There is a lot of creative energy going on around you. I also think you should start doing some business around this project even though it is not finished yet."

"What do you mean?" I asked Lexa.

"Well, since you already published a few essays that are part of the book, why can't you start contacting some agents?"

"I guess I'm hesitant because I don't know how it ends," I said.

After she finished that positive layout, I shuffled and cut the cards again and we moved onto the subject of relationships. Lexa was impressed when I told her I was dating.

"That's a huge change," she said, noting the cards indicated my social life was picking up. "But there is still some residue from your marriage that needs to be reckoned with. Truthfully, I don't see you being in a relationship until you finish drafting this book project. You still aren't ready."

"Really?" I said, thinking that her interpretation would motivate me to churn out pages.

"You're busy and committed to the writing," she continued. "It's hard to be searching for love when you already have this other commitment, so you are dating to give yourself energy and even material," she laughed.

"I'm not ready because my heart is still hung up, or I'm too busy writing?"

"Both," she said. "But by dating different women you grow and your criteria changes When I say there is residue, it's like something has ended or you have outgrown it, but you are still operating with that old system. Once you make this last transition, you will find someone compatible."

"I see what you mean about criteria. I haven't dated anyone in a long time and dating in your sixties is very different than dating in your thirties. It's been good for me and gives me confidence, but it would be nice to have a girlfriend and some sex."

"I did not say you were not going to have sex," she said, studying the cards.

"Well okay! That's good news."

"You could have a lot of sex or a little sex," Lexa said. "But it may not lead to a relationship. It's fun, exploratory. Basically you're entering the kissing a lot of frogs stage. I don't see you getting married for a while—at least six months."

Of course, as a devotee of readings, I knew the timeline was the least accurate area, the hardest to predict. I asked if she saw places where I should be going to meet people.

"Let's do another layout," she said as she swept up the cards and handed them to me. "Shuffle and give me seven."

"Okay. This layout says that as long as you're connected to people, it's good." Lexa advised me to stay on one dating site, not to scatter my energy, but she suggested I join some meet-up groups related to my interests.

"I was thinking of doing that too."

"A lot of things are changing for you and don't be surprised if you go through a phase where nobody looks good, but that's okay. It means you are in the thick of your transition and after crossing through that you'll be in the right time and right place for another relationship to happen."

I came out of the reading determined to kiss a lot of frogs, crank out the pages, and make this final transition happen. I felt reassured I was on the right path.

About three weeks after my dinner with Paul, I got an e-mail from Chaz, the cop, introducing herself. Based upon what she wrote, Paul had already told her I did not want to date a police officer. I felt a little bad about that, but it was the truth.

I asked Chaz to send a picture, and she seemed pretty attractive. From the e-mails we exchanged I learned she had two adult daughters and three grandkids. Based upon everyone's ages, she had her daughters in her early twenties. I assumed she'd been married and divorced but did not ask. Nor did I ask when she came out. Chaz told me she became a cop in her late twenties to have a steady salary to take care of her kids. Our early lives could not have been more different. She was an officer of the law. I was a hippie teacher who invented a class called Contemporary Lyrical Verse, where students analyzed rock songs.

And our current lives seemed different too. She liked golfing and cooking and taking care of her house and doing yard work. She seemed very suburban, while I was urban to the core. What was it with all the Jersey dykes and golf? I had never played golf in my life. I didn't enjoy cooking, and lived in a tiny studio where the super fixed things.

I was searching for some common ground—other than the fact that we were both single gay women in the same age bracket. I found out we both loved the beach and she liked to read. I was surprised to discover she too had a master's degree and had been studying to become a teacher, except she did not work in education. She had been a cop for the past thirty years while I'd been a writer and teacher. One thing Chaz had in her favor was that she was a water sign and the tarot card reader, Roland, had told me that the woman coming into my life was a water sign.

After the transformative Labor Day weekend chanting at Omega I felt sure I had put Slim in the past. She no longer had my heart or mind, but maybe what Lexa meant by "residue" was that I using my ex as my criteria for a new mate. I wanted a hip downtown artist.

Since Chaz seemed eager to meet me, I agreed to get together. I wanted to practice being open. And I still had not kissed anyone, and I needed to bring on the frogs.

"Am I using baddar?" I asked my therapist when I told her the latest.

"Yes, you have a stereotype," said Dr. R. "I used to know a cop who was cool. What's her name?"

"Chaz"

"Oh, sexy name," said my shrink. "You have to meet to see if you have enough in common. You both like gardening."

"She grows vegetables in her backyard. I tend a flower box in front of my building," I retorted. "I don't spend my weekends raking leaves or whatever they do in suburbia."

"My wife likes yard work and I think it's boring," said Dr. R. " You don't have to have the same interests as…"

"Your wife?" I said, surprised. "I didn't know you two had gotten married.

Congratulations."

"Thanks," said Dr. R. "Actually, I hate the term wife, but if I say spouse or partner, it is gender neutral, so…"

I was on a roll and quickly got back to the topic: "Being in law enforcement is a big negative for me. That line of work is about controlling people's behavior," I said, recalling how Slim was almost trampled by a police horse when she was covering a demonstration. "My work helps people expand their minds."

"Maybe she sees her work as keeping the world safe," said Dr. R. "You have an opportunity to see if your stereotype is correct."

"Okay, Okay, I'm going to meet her," I said. "But why is a cop interested in me? Why can't someone more like me be interested in me?"

"Someone more like you can be a bitch," Dr. R. said.

I knew exactly who she meant.

"And somebody who is a cop can be multifaceted," Dr. R. said. "You are prejudiced."

"True," I admitted, feeling a bit bad because Chaz was clearly pursuing me, which felt flattering. Or maybe it was just her cop training kicking in—to go after the prey. No matter what I wrote her about how our lifestyles seemed opposite, she still wanted to meet me.

"Look, she finds you interesting so she must think you have something in common," said my therapist. "She sounds intellectually inclined and like she took that job for the money."

I was the type of person who prided herself on never taking jobs just for the money, but then I never had children to support and I was broke until recently.

We spent the rest of the session discussing a dream where I went to work half-undressed and then a new teacher stole my class roster to see how to set it up. When I called him on this act, he poked me between the eyes, where the third eye is located.

"Dating is putting yourself in a position where you don't have any control," said Dr. R. "and that is what the dream represents. It is about opening your heart. It's scary and the baddar tries to protect you because you feel vulnerable."

After I spoke with my therapist, I was discussing dating with Kurt, my gay male office mate, who also wanted to meet someone. I expressed reservations about the cop.

"Oh, I'd love to date a cop," said Kurt. "That sounds so sexy."

"Do you like men in uniforms?" I asked.

"Well, the last man in uniform I was attracted to was the exterminator," he said.

"The exterminator?" I laughed, as I left to teach a class.

Chaz was early, sitting on a bench outside Café Condesa.

"You must be Chaz," I said extending my hand. My immediate take was that she looked better in the photos. Her face was more lined than I expected, and her thick lenses enlarged her brown eyes. She had mousy brown hair, but she was trim and fit, as Paul had described.

"Hi. This is for you," she said handing me fresh-cut mums and a bag of arugula. "From my garden."

"Thanks. That's very sweet," I said as we entered the restaurant and found a table.

Chaz seemed nervous as we sat down. She immediately pulled out a copy of an essay she'd printed from my website. "I've got bunch of questions about this," she said.

She'd underlined a few sentences. Talk about a close reading. I'd written this over a year ago and didn't remember it that well. When we chatted on e-mail, Chaz had asked about my work and I'd sent her a link and mentioned a few essays she might want to read. I'd decided people reading my work beforehand was okay, as long as I knew about it.

The conversation began with her telling me how much she related to this section about growing and expanding since my breakup with Slim. Of course, I liked to get compliments about my writing, but Chaz used this to segue into a discussion of how her fifteen-year relationship ended two years and three months ago. I was waiting to hear how many hours.

"Hold on a second," I said in an futile effort to derail this direction. "You know my name but I don't know your last name, and I'm guessing Chaz is a nickname."

"My full name is Donna Chazinski. Chaz comes from my last name."

"That is so butch," I slipped. It also sounded juvenile or collegiate. When my brother was in college, a few of his friends called him "Walt," a shortened version of our last name. As soon as that comment popped out of my mouth, I knew I needed to turn down the baddar.

Chaz circled back to rehashing her breakup, as if she'd found a kindred soul who would understand. Slim and I had broken up over four years ago. Was I still obsessing two years ago? Absolutely, which was why I'd only started dating in the past six months and why I found Chaz annoying. She was not ready and seemed unconscious of this. When the server came to take our orders, she hadn't even glanced at the menu. We ordered wine and asked the waitress to return.

"Wasn't it a shock that the person you thought you'd spend the rest of your life with left?" she asked.

"Well, sure," I said. "But looking back there were clues."

"Bet it hurt a lot to be left after twenty-six years," she probed.

I did not think this line was appropriate first date conversation. Why would I want to revisit this painful chapter with someone I just met? I had to assume Chaz hadn't dated much since her breakup and she was still processing it. To a lesser degree, I was too, but I did most of my work with my therapist. Chaz's only stint in analysis was when she and her ex saw a straight male shrink for two years.

"And we still broke up," Chaz said, "after doing all that work. I always thought he was on her side," she said.

"Why didn't you see a lesbian therapist for couples counseling?" I asked.

"Easier to do when you live in Manhattan," she said.

I though it was bizarre when Chaz said they never fought in fifteen years together. "Are you serious?" I said. I knew I fought excessively with Slim, but never fighting seemed unhealthy too.

The most interesting thing I learned was that Chaz's ex had bolted in a similar manner. Like Slim, she did not meet anyone new. But she wanted to see what she had missed because this had been her only major same-sex relationship. Chaz's ex worked in finance and insisted they buy a big house in suburbia, which Chaz got stuck with after their breakup. Made me glad Slim and I never owned any property together.

"Enough of the ex talk," I said when our entrees arrived, but she did not pick up my hint. After a while I gave in and went along. I found myself talking more about Slim than on all my recent dates combined. I usually got into it only if the other person asked; I certainly never led off with this topic. But even then I was guarded about what I revealed. Much of what I said had been in print, had already been filtered for public consumption. Chaz seemed to have no boundaries. She even told me her ex's pet name!

Although the bulk of the conversation was about our breakups, Chaz showed an interest in my creative work. She even asked questions about my writing process. This allowed me to entertain the idea that I did not have to be with a fellow artist to find someone who got me and my creative drive and need for solitude.

From an earlier email, I knew that Chaz was checking out a retirement community in Toms River. Good Lord, I had thought when I read this. Shoot me if I ever land up in a place like that before I'm 90. My mother was now 88 and lived on her own and ran two households. I wanted to be like her, though I envisioned getting old in Westbeth, which even had an onsite social worker for the seniors. I also thought if you were going to move to a retirement community, why not go all the way and move to Florida and avoid winter?

"Why Toms River?" I asked when she'd mentioned visiting the place recently. "You know Ocean County is very Republican except for the summer people."

"We can change that," she said. "If enough of us move there."

At least she wasn't Republican, but I still did not get why anyone wanted to live in that area. The nearest gay bar was in the next county, twenty miles away in Asbury Park.

"Have you considered other places?" I asked.

"I do like Rehoboth Beach in Delaware," she said.

"That's a cool town and very gay-friendly. Why not retire there?" I asked, relieved we were no longer talking about the exes.

"Too far from my parents who live in upstate New York. I need to be within five or six hours of them. They told me Toms River was the limit."

"What?" I asked, shocked a fifty-eight-year-old woman would let her parents dictate the geographic parameters of her retirement.

"I promised to take care of them when they get old," she said.

"Well, that's nice," I said. "But they chose to stay up there when you've been in New Jersey all these years. Why must you accommodate their choice?"

"I had a "Leave It to Beaver" childhood," she said, as if that explained her controlling parents and her overattachment.

"I thought I had a "Leave It to Beaver" childhood too," I said snarkily, "until I got into psychotherapy."

Thankfully, the food was delicious and the wine was excellent. I had the artichoke ravioli with a red sauce laced with olives. Chaz raved about the salmon with a special salsa. I could always count on Café Condesa for a good experience, even if the date was going haywire. Chaz wanted to grab the check but I insisted we split it. After all the ex talk, I felt more like I was with a friend rehashing a group therapy session than on a first date.

We left the restaurant and I guided her through the confusing street grid of the West Village to the Cubbyhole. "You sure know your way around this neighborhood," she said as I zigzagged through the slow-moving tourists.

I forgot the Cubbyhole would be mobbed. That's why locals seldom went there on the weekend—too many bridge and tunnel people (like my date). So we headed back toward Rubyfruit. As we strolled along Hudson Street her loping gait was very butch. I could just picture her in uniform with a gun in her holster.

Inside the club, we landed downstairs on a couch. She bought me a beer and started up with the ex talk again. Had there been any sparks, this recurrent topic would have doused them. We did not stay long because she had to get up early the next day. I walked her to her car and we hugged good night. She told me she had two cars, whereas, I had not owned one since I moved from New Jersey to Manhattan thirty-five years ago. I used public transportation.

The next day I called Paul, the matchmaker, and griped, "She is so not over her ex and she's too hooked into her parents. I'd never let my mother tell me where I can or can't live. But she seems like a nice person."

"Sorry," said Paul, "she's a sweet person but she's a country bumpkin who landed in New Jersey. I knew this was a long shot." Paul and I both grew up in gritty Paterson.

"Well, thanks for thinking of me," I said. "I'd be curious to hear her take."

The next day Paul called. "I told her what you said about too much ex talk," he said.

"I hope that did not hurt her feelings," I said.

"She needs to hear that," he said. "It's not a good dating strategy."

"What did she say about me?" I asked.

"She thought you were attractive," he said. "But too New York for her."

21

OLD FRIENDS:
SEPTEMBER 2010

While my building prepared for its fortieth anniversary as an arts complex, I was heading out to New Jersey for the homecoming at my Catholic college. I had graduated forty years ago (when the school was all women), and two of my sorority sisters contacted me about going. I thought it would be a hoot. We planned to do our own thing, picking and choosing events. We were not going to the luncheon or the Mass at Rosary Hall.

What really triggered our private reunion was that my friends, Rosina and Angela, were art majors and their former professor and mentor, Sister Gerardine, an eighty-eight-year-old nun, was having a retrospective of her life work. They both wanted to attend the opening. Two other old friends, Marian and Adriana, would be meeting us on campus. Rosina was flying in from Northern California and staying with Angela in Morristown. They each called me and said, "You have to come."

I not only wanted to see my dear friends, but I thought reconnecting with people who knew me when I was young—uncovering my former self—might be the final steps in my healing process. Digging back into my early life might give me an added perspective.

So on a gorgeous late September Saturday, I took a train from Penn Station to Convent Station. As I stepped off the train, Rosina was standing by the track waving and came running to greet me. I'd seen her a few years ago when she was in New York. She was trim but her face was lined around her mouth, probably because she still smoked cigarettes.

LOOKING FOR A KISS

Angela stood near her car grinning. Angela had gained over ten pounds but she looked as beautiful as I recalled. Dark hair, dark eyes, just an older version. We'd last seen each other thirty years ago at our ten-year sorority reunion.

"Oh my God, Kate, you look fantastic," said Angela. "What a nice complexion."

"You know what I just realized," I said as I settled into Angela's car. "I'm the only non-Italian in our little party, the only one whose last name does not end in a vowel."

"Then girl, prepared to be overwhelmed," Rosina said as we took off and all burst out laughing. "This day is gonna be like that movie the Banger Sisters, but we are calling ourselves the Shit Upon Sisters because we have all been dumped upon."

"You're too much," I said recalling how Rosina used to crack us up in the student lounge with her imitations of Gilda Radner doing Emily Litella, the mixed-up Italian TV critic. Both she and Angela knew about my gay divorce from Slim who Rosina had met and never liked. Rosina was divorced three times and struggling to make a living as a tile artist in Northern California. She was a gifted artist but not good at marketing herself.

Angela was a widow whose husband had hidden a lot from her: his drinking problem (which caused his premature death) and the fact that they were bankrupt. She had to sell their huge home, where they raised five children, downscale into a condo and find a job. She now taught art in a high school and was dating on the Internet, something we had in common today.

"Looks like Marian is the only one of us not divorced," said Rosina.

"True," I said. "They have been together like forty years, but when we spoke on the phone, she told me her husband had an affair and they went to counseling. But you did not hear that from me."

"Okay so she qualifies as shit-upon," said Rosina. "She's in the club."

"What about Adriana?" I asked, knowing she and Angela had been friends since seventh grade. They both grew up in Newark in prominent local families.

"She has been through a lot too," said Angela. "First, that bastard Bobby walked out and left her with three little kids."

"I remember him," I said. "They were engaged senior year."

"I thought she'd have a breakdown, but her parents helped her out," added

Angela. "Then she married this wonderful man and they blended their families. But he got sick and died about eight years ago."

"Oh *marone*," said Rosina, as we began a day where conversations would be laced with Italian words, as my Jewish friends in the city threw Yiddish expressions into the mix. My speech pattern was less colorful.

"Wow. She's had it rough," I said, thinking my life had less tragedy.

"But she is loaded," said Angela, who was destitute after her husband died.

As we drove onto the leafy campus and parked near the new arts complex, I saw several other new buildings, including a large student center with a gymnasium. I recognized Rosary Hall and the library, which still looked stately and gothic. But the biggest shock was seeing male students on campus.

The opening was packed, and Sister Gerardine was thrilled to see my friends, her star pupils, who had flowers for her. I photographed the three of them with Sister's sculptures in the background. As we were checking out the art—lots of stained glass with religious themes—our friend Marian arrived. She was still plump, still had blonde streaks in her hair, but now she had a nose ring. We all hugged and I took more pictures. Marian was retired and dabbled in real estate.

Just as we were about to leave and walk around the campus, Adriana finally arrived. More hugs. It figures that the one who lived ten minutes from campus got there the latest. I had not seen her since graduation and she looked stunning—great figure and cool haircut, much better than the flip she wore during college. She was a runner and a history teacher. I gave someone my camera to capture us all.

After the opening, the five of us drove back in a little caravan to Angela's condo where she hung the sorority banner in her dining room. "Can't believe I still have this," she said.

Her dining room had beautiful china cabinets and the place settings were perfect. It was so obvious she was a great homemaker. The four of us gathered around her table as Angela took plates of antipasto and grilled eggplant out of her refrigerator. We nibbled on the appetizers as Angela put out a big salad and heated up rigatoni with a delicious mushroom cream sauce.

"*Mangia*," she told us as she sat down to join us.

"Let's have a toast," said Rosina, who'd opened bottles of red and white wine and poured everyone a glass. "Here's to us and to the girls of Tau Omega Kappa."

"To us. *Salud*," said Marian and we all clinked glasses.

After dinner, we drank beer and more wine and looked at the old yearbook, finding all our pictures and wondering about former classmates as we flipped through the pages.

"Can you believe Jenny, the biggest druggie on campus, became born again?" I asked. This was old news I'd heard from Rosina but I was not sure if everyone knew it.

"And she told me Kate was going to hell for being gay," added Rosina.

"Get out," said Adriana. "Didn't she have a love child right after graduation? And gave him some weird name—"

"Yeah, but then she switched it to some Christian name," supplied Rosina.

"She did too many heavy drugs," said Angela as she took out a canister with marijuana and asked Rosina to roll a joint.

"Where did you get that?" asked Adriana, shocked. Angela rarely got high in college.

"From my son-in-law," said Angela, as the joint went around.

Adriana abstained and so did Marian who used to be a big pothead and said she could not believe we were still doing this at 60.

"Why not?" said Angela as Marian shook her head in disbelief. "Doctor's orders," quipped Angela, who had multiple sclerosis and was now walking with a cane.

"Remember this girl," said Marian pointing to a picture. "What a *puttana*. She had, like, three abortions."

"And she was pregnant when we graduated," I said.

"Did I tell you what happened to Lisa," said Adriana as we flipped to the page with Lisa's photo. "I saw her working in Pathmark bagging groceries. She said hello to me and I felt embarrassed for her."

"Oh, that is sad," I said. "I wonder how she landed up there."

"I heard she drinks too much," said Rosina.

"Does anyone remember this girl Carmen Marcone? asked Angela. "She was a year or two behind us. I want to find her."

"Look in the back of the yearbook," said Rosina. "There is a directory of all the classes."

"What's with this Carmen?" asked Adriana.

"Angela wants to fix her up with Kate," said Marian.

"Huh?" said Adriana, puzzled.

"Tell her the story," I said to Angela. The rest of us had heard it earlier that day.

When we were juniors, Angela had befriended this student who was crying in the cafeteria because her aunt had just died. Angela sat with her and bought her ice cream and held her hand while she sobbed. This sounded typical because Angela was always compassionate and sweet. After that, they chatted whenever running into each other on campus. Years after we graduated, Carmen looked up Angela, then married, and visited her. Carmen told Angela she was gay and confessed she had been in love with her the entire time.

"This woman was gorgeous," Angela added, "dark hair, very petite. But I have to tell you, Kate, she's not as smart as you. She's a little *stoonad* but very nice."

Adriana had opened up Angela's lap top and started searching. "She's not on Facebook and Google has nothing. I'll try the phone directory. Where did she live?"

"South Orange," said Rosina, looking at the yearbook. "But that was forty years ago."

The whole exercise was silly, but I was touched that my sorority sisters were trying to fix me up with another woman. I was still seeing men when I was in college. These women really were my sisters. I first met them when I was seventeen. Now I was I was sixty-one. They loved me when I was straight and now they loved me as a lesbian.

When we talked about dating, I felt young again. Our conversation flowed as if we'd just seen each other in the grungy basement lounge after a midterm. Except now Angela and Adriana were grandmothers who lapsed into grandkid talk. When Rosina rolled her eyes, Adriana said, "No more grandkid stories, after this one."

The rest of us never had children. With the exception of Marian, we'd all been divorced or widowed and had relationships that ended badly. Catholic college had not taught us how to find eternal mates. We never found Carmen on the Internet, but someone suggested the alumni office. Angela, the matchmaker, vowed to go that route.

Adriana and Marian left at nine o'clock because they had to get up early the next day. Adriana, who looked very fit, was volunteering at a charity run. As we

LOOKING FOR A KISS

hugged goodbye in the driveway, Adriana said, "Let's not wait another forty years to get together."

Marian was driving back to South Carolina where she and her husband had retired. I used to hang with them at the Jersey Shore. Both natives, she said they were "done with New Jersey." Marian had come up the day before and stayed at her sister's place. As we said goodbye, I over-heard her say to Rosina, who seldom got to the East Coast, "I'll probably never see you again."

The three of us went back to the table and noshed on snacks. Around ten o'clock, Angela and Rosina took me to the train station to catch the 10:24 back into Penn Station. We hugged goodbye, with me screaming, "Love you guys." Angela promised to visit me in the city, where her three sons lived. Her youngest had just gotten his first role on Broadway. I had renewed a friendship with an old friend who could become a new friend. Angela seemed cooler now than when she was in college under the thumb of an overprotective father. Rosina was always asking me to visit in California but I hadn't gone West in years.

I was hoping to nap during the hour-long ride back, but no such luck. These rowdy drunk women were carrying on, singing loudly and off-key, "You've got a friend." I gave up on sleeping and let myself bask in warm feelings of reconnecting with old friends who made me feel loved. I daydreamed and recalled myself when I was in college, still straight.

22

BLASTED BACK INTO THE PAST:
1967-1975

During my sophomore year at the Catholic women's college, I had sex with Bob, a boyfriend I met during my last few months of high school. Bob had transferred into my class after getting kicked out of a ritzy academy. We'd broken up after a year of going steady but got back together for a sex date because we both were embarrassed to be virgins at eighteen. Bob called me up, wanting to know if I had "done it" yet with anyone. I confessed I had not "done it" and he also admitted his inexperience, so we agreed to have sex that Saturday night. I wanted to get this over with and figured Bob was a good choice. He was very funny and I trusted him.

We both still lived at home and could not afford a motel, so Bob suggested we fuck in the office of the literary magazine on the campus of St. Peter's College in Jersey City. He was an editor and had a key to a funky room with big desks, file cabinets, and typewriters.

I'm not sure if I was nervous about the sex or about getting caught or both. Although Bob assured me that no one would come barging into the locked office, he insisted we keep the lights off for fear this might alert a security guard. I smashed my knee into a bulky metal desk as he led me across the room to a space on the floor. "Oww! I can't see in here," I said.

We drank some cheap red wine, lit a candle, and took off our clothes. We had sex on a blanket we threw on the hard office floor. It was fast, painful, boring. Not like the movies. The room was freezing, so we hurried to get dressed again. At least I was not a virgin anymore. I expected to feel differently but I just felt relieved it was over.

LOOKING FOR A KISS

My first two years of college were a blitz of beer parties, new friends, and dates with guys whose efforts to grope me were a turn off. It never occurred to me I was more attracted to my female friends. I was supposed to feel passion toward men, like my sorority sisters described, but I didn't. I knew if I wanted to keep a guy I should follow Rosina's advice: "You have to suck their dicks." The thought of doing that made me gag.

When I slept with men, I never liked how penises looked or how they felt when I touched them. I managed to have several boyfriends without giving blow jobs. They got on top of me and ejaculated. I didn't like it, but I didn't know any better. I didn't like male bodies in general—their bigness, their hairiness, their scratchy faces. I never had oral sex with a man. They never offered and I never asked.

During the six years I slept with men, from 1968 to 1974, I did not think I was a lesbian. It did not even dawn on me. I just thought the sex was bad. Or I hadn't met the right guy. Then again, my main college and postcollege boyfriend, Joe, was a closeted gay man. I was relieved he did not pressure me into sleeping with him more than once a week.

I had nothing against men. I admired my handsome English teacher father—he was a role model. I was close to my brother John when we were growing up. I've always had male friends. I just didn't jive with men as sexual partners. I later realized women had the right apparatus for me—soft skin, breasts, and a vagina. Plus, they thought with their hearts and minds, not their cocks.

During my freshman year, I checked out various sororities, including Tau Omega Kappa. The girls in TOK were cute and sassy and liked to party. "You don't want to join them," an upperclassman warned me, as we sat in the dank basement lounge smoking cigarettes. "All they do is drink and smoke pot." Sounded like fun to me. I went to the rush tea, got asked to pledge. Right away, I was more popular than in high school where I was not in the A-list cheerleader crowd.

Saturday nights, my girl friends and I went to parties at fraternity houses from men's colleges. Caldwell College girls hung out with Seton Hall guys. We drank beer from kegs and smoked and danced to Motown: the Temptations' "Cloud Nine" and the Supremes' "Love Child." I drank too much and shouldn't have been driving home. One night, I stopped on windy Valley Road, my head spinning, pulled to the curbside, opened the car door, and threw up. I got blasted every weekend.

By my junior year, I was seriously depressed. Class work seemed overwhelming and living at home with my conservative Catholic parents was stifling. I dated guys but didn't connect with them the way my girlfriends described. I hadn't yet realized I was different. I considered dropping out, but feared I would never get out of my hometown. The college had no counseling. My parents sent me to the family doctor who wrote a prescription for an antidepressant that I never took. No one suggested therapy. One poem I wrote for the campus magazine described feeling split off from myself. A snotty sorority sister (not invited to our little reunion) bluntly told me, "If that's how you feel, you're fucked up."

Nothing lifted my mood until I started dating Joe. The sex was not good, but he was a lifeline out of my depression and my guide into the radical '60s. We met at the Jersey Shore during the East Coast summer of love—1968—when my sorority rented a summer house in beach party town Belmar. Joe's best friend Tommy was dating a sister, and every Saturday, the guys drove over to visit.

Joe liked it when I was at the house because I brought cool records—Jimi Hendrix, Blood, Sweat, and Tears, the Electric Flag. I liked it when Joe was at the house because he brought pot. We did not date that summer; we just hung out. That fall, he took off cross-country a la *Easy Rider*. Joe sent me a postcard from Monterey and we got together after he returned.

Joe was older than I, already out of college. I was only a junior. Joe had his own apartment, a motorcycle, and long hair. My father disliked him. It didn't help that my mother found my birth control pills when snooping in my dresser. Joe said he liked me as soon as he read the bumper sticker on my car: "Stick it in your ear."

When I began dating Joe, he was a reporter at the *Paterson News*. He covered my hometown and freelanced as the music editor for the *Aquarian*, the alternative newspaper based in Montclair. Since he got press passes, we were regulars at the Capitol Theatre in Passaic and the Fillmore East in the Village. Joe got me started writing professionally. He had read my reviews in the campus paper and I became the initial female rock critic for the *Aquarian*.

When I returned for my senior year of college, everyone on campus was impressed that Joe and I had gone to Woodstock. At my conservative college, I often felt like an oddball, but when I came back to campus for my last year, I felt very cool. At Woodstock I hung out with thousands of kids like me. I was not a misfit. I was just enrolled in the wrong school. I left the festival feeling elated. We could change the world, rearrange the world, just like Crosby, Stills and Nash sang. Something inside me had shifted and I felt powerful.

In the spring of 1972, two years after I graduated college, Joe ended our three-and-a-half-year relationship. We were in the woods, sitting alongside a brook when he told me he liked men, that he did not want to keep stringing me along, pretending he liked women.

"What?" I screamed, "You told me I was cute."

"You are cute and you look like a guy from the back, so that attracted me. And I like you as a person. I'm sorry I deceived you. I got out of the draft for Vietnam, by telling that shrink I'm gay. Didn't you wonder how I got out?"

"I knew you were seeing a shrink, but . . . How long have you known this about yourself?" I was fuming.

"Probably all my life, when I was a little kid and I saw this movie starring Frank Sinatra. I was so turned on to him."

"I can't fucking believe this," I shouted, glad we were isolated.

"Kate," Joe called, as I walked away. "I hope we can be friends again, after you stop being mad at me."

I was shocked. How could I not have known? Was that why the sex was not good? What did he mean I looked like a guy? While I was dating Joe, I spent weekends at the hippie house where he lived on Lake Valhalla in Montville. That's where Joe and Tommy and I had a threesome. Dopey me. I had no idea Joe was in love with Tommy, who agreed because he wanted to get it on with me. Joe got to stare at naked Tommy making love to his girlfriend (the guys didn't do anything together), and I got to have sex with my closeted lover's hot best friend.

After Joe came out, I went to California that summer to visit Rosina, who had moved to Marin County after graduation. I needed to get off the East Coast for the first time in my life and try to figure out what was going on. Why had I spent over three years with a gay guy? When I returned to New Jersey, I moved out of my parents' home and into "Rock Hill" as an earlier sign had dubbed the lake house.

It was rustic stone country house built in the 1940s. Roomy and private, its sun porch overlooked the lake, which we could see in winter when the trees in front were bare. The house had four bedrooms, two on each floor, and a huge stone fireplace in the living room with a cathedral ceiling of pine beams. I had the dormer ceiling attic room, the coziest bedroom, just big enough for a water bed, table and chair.

Soon Joe introduced us to Anthony, his first serious boyfriend. He was younger, only 19, and lived at home in Paramus. When his father discovered the relationship, he was enraged and threatened to kill "that faggot pervert" with a gun. When Joe told us, he was still our roommate, waiting to move into his new apartment—an uncomfortable, unplanned two-month overlap with my arrival. My room was upstairs, across the hall from his. My roommates, Jim and Gary, had larger bedrooms downstairs.

"Does Anthony's father know where you live?" Jim asked.

"Yeah, he found a letter with my return address."

"Oh great," Jim said. "Your boyfriend's father, who's probably in the mob, knows you live here and wants you dead."

"Come on," said Joe. "Don't assume he's in the mob just because he's Italian and lives in New Jersey."

"And owns a construction company," Gary finished.

Jim suggested putting signs on the doors, so he would not get bumped off by mistake: "Upstairs to Joe's room."

"Make sure the signs say 'turn right at the top of the stairs,'" I added. "I wouldn't want the hit man coming upstairs and going into my room."

"Not funny," Joe said. We were scared for him and relieved when he moved out.

I basked in my idyllic life in the lake house doing yoga on the sun porch and learning Transcendental Meditation. Joe dropped by on weekends to visit with his gay friends. He had exchanged his Mick Jagger worship for David Bowie glitter. Suddenly, I knew gay people, but they were all males, including several former students.

Although I continued to sleep with men, I soon became curious about women. There had to be a reason I never got off with men. Joe and Anthony invited me to meet them at the M&K disco in Asbury Park. Asbury always had a gay scene.

Saturday night, August 1974. The M&K was a tan building on Cookman Avenue, a seedy old hotel that housed a three-story club. It was a resort with rooms

LOOKING FOR A KISS

to let and a cruisy gay pool scene. Joe and Anthony rented a suite for the weekend and invited me to crash there if I was too tired or too drunk to drive back that night.

The first floor was mixed, men and women; the second floor was men; the third floor was women. I left Joe and Anthony and ventured to the dyke floor. I was scared but excited. This felt bold. I got picked up fast by a cute bleached blond named Tania. She was in the Navy and lived at the nearby base. She wasn't from this area and had come to the disco with her Navy pals. She had been out a while. I figured it made sense to do it with an experienced woman. So what if Tania had a girl in every port. We danced, got drunk, and decided to get a room in the M&K.

I wanted to lose my queer virginity. I knew something was off in my sex life. I used to think that was because Joe was the wrong type (he was dark, hairy, chubby, and I liked men who were thin and smooth), but maybe he was the wrong gender for me and vice versa.

Since I was totally inexperienced, I was passive and let Tania take the lead. I can't remember much because I was drunk. She was attractive and I liked whatever she did. I liked that there was no penis and no cum. I liked how her face felt so soft.

Now I wanted to have sex with a woman I clicked with. Tania called after our night of sex in the sleazy hotel. She asked me out for the next weekend. I knew I did not want to pursue a relationship with her; we had little in common. I was an East Coast college grad who had protested the draft. She was a high school grad who'd enlisted in the service to escape Oklahoma. I don't remember what I said on the phone, except that I'd had a good time. After my adventure at the M&K disco, I thought I might be bisexual, so I continued halfheartedly sleeping with men, including a cute colleague who was my type—blond hair, blue eyes, thin, tight ass. But he did nothing for me sexually. So it was not about body type. That's when I decided to seek lesbians more like the men I dated. Smart. Readers. Writers.

A few months later, I came out with Libby. Dear, sweet, delicious Libby. She was a younger woman who attended parties in the hippie house when I lived there. She had gone to an alternative high school where Joe and Tommy had been teachers. After Libby left for college in Boston, Joe reported that she had become a lesbian feminist. I always liked Libby and that news intrigued me. When she returned home unexpectedly, taking off a semester after a bad breakup, Joe suggested we all meet at this gay bar in Hackensack, probably a mafia dive. It was right before Christmas and the place was decorated with tacky holiday lights.

I had forgotten Libby was short—a little over five feet. Short and very cute—brown eyes, curly brown hair, nice smile. She was trim with firm breasts, not flat-chested like some other women who are small. We hugged. I was attracted to her.

We found a table, ordered some beers, started talking about her courses, what she was reading, what I was reading. She was a women's studies major, taking classes in history and literature and gender theory. Classes like that were not even offered at my women's colleges five years earlier. Libby and I discussed feminist poets—Adrienne Rich, Anne Sexton, June Jordan, Audre Lorde—but I could not keep up with the political stuff; she was fluent in feminist theory.

Joe disappeared to shoot pool, even though he never played pool. I asked Libby about being a dyke, knowing that Joe had filled her in that I was experimenting with women. I felt like a complete idiot.

"Like how did you know?"

"You'll just know," she smiled. "In the meanwhile, I'm gonna get you a copy of *Sappho Was a Right-On Woman.*"

"Great, thanks." I had read *Sisterhood Is Powerful,* so I passed that test, but I had never read an exclusively lesbian book. We did not go home together that night, but we made a date for the next Saturday. The attraction was so intense I was burning up inside all week.

When we did get it on, I was completely turned on during our lovemaking. I wanted her body and her touch. I was hungry for her mouth and her breasts. I did not want to get out of bed with her, even for food. Libby was beautiful, young, angelic looking—especially when lying asleep on the pillow. I fell in love. I ached with desire. And I knew.

Our affair was wildly impractical. Libby was only nineteen, a college student; I was twenty-five and had a career as a high school teacher. Libby was smart and well read, a feisty lesbian feminist, but we were in different places in our lives. When she broke up with me, after a few torrid months, I was devastated and burned her letters in the fireplace—a dramatic act I regretted later.

After our affair ended, I knew that I wanted to be involved with women. While we broke up before "lesbian bed death" had a chance to set in, I'd never felt that way about any man.

LOOKING FOR A KISS

I finally realized that I was gay, always had been, but never figured it out it until then. I thought about how I'd never get married, never have kids. I felt sad. I felt relieved. So many things made sense for the first time. When my grammar school friend Kathy and I played house, I always wanted to be the father. Being the mother was boring, stuck in the room playing with baby dolls. The father went into the world and he got to wear a jacket and tie.

I'd hated frilly feminine clothes and always wanted what my mother called "man-tailored shirts." My favorite clothing from junior high school was my unisex striped beatnik sweater. I had never liked girly things—party dresses and high heels. My friend Rosina once asked me why I dressed so androgynous.

After coming out to myself, I wanted to be as out as possible. I wanted to be around gay women. I wanted to be out at work. The Monday I returned to my classroom after a hot weekend in bed with Libby (right before she ended things), I was washing my face in the faculty bathroom and wondering if I looked differently. Would my students see a lavender "L"?

This was the mid-70s, way before Melissa Etheridge sang, "Yes, I Am." As I trotted off to meet my first period English class, I kept thinking of a recent discussion about gay rights, where an honor student said if she heard I was gay (she was being hypothetical but amazingly prescient), it would be the only thing she could think about during class. *How distracting*, I thought. Forget Hester Prynne. I would be more scandalous.

I could not imagine being out in the classroom at this time, and I didn't want this to become an issue for my father, who worked in this same school system. I was not as brave as the dyke daughter of the Spanish teacher, who sat in the faculty room smoking a pipe. But she was only a sub, not a full-timer. Suddenly I realized there were other gay and lesbian teachers, but all deeply in the closet. If I made friendly overtures, they changed the subject.

Less than a year after coming out, I bolted to the city. During the mid-70s, I could not imagine being queer and living in New Jersey; plus, I always loved the Village. Now I had the impetus to move. So I decamped into Manhattan alone after living cozily with three friendly roommates. I left my secure job as a high school English teacher and a spacious country home and moved to a railroad flat to be a Village dyke. All I knew was that I had to do it. I felt sad and scared and excited at the same time. I gave up a four-bedroom lakeside house with a fireplace and shady private terrace for a walk-up tenement with a bathtub in the kitchen.

When I moved to the East Village in 1975, it was not a safe neighborhood. Peace and love had faded. Heroin had arrived. But the area was all I could afford and it was within walking distance to the women's bars. Bonnie & Clyde's, a basement dive, became my main hangout; the college-educated dykes flocked there to talk politics. I felt like I had arrived; my new life as a gay woman was beginning.

The apartment was a sublet, so I could see if I'd like Manhattan. I had no idea I'd spend the next two decades living in the East Village. I gave up my place in the hippie house and sold my green Volkswagen beetle. I was not rushing back to New Jersey. Within a year after I moved, Joe got a job in the city and found an apartment on the Upper West Side.

No question that Joe played a big role in my evolution. As my hippie boyfriend, he had rescued me from the insular world of a conservative Catholic women's college, and as my gay male pal, he helped me come out.

When Joe died of AIDS in 1989 at 43, his Italian Catholic mother arranged the service at his boyhood church in New Jersey. The priest who spoke had never met Joe and kept referring to him as Joseph. "I was told Joseph loved the ocean, and he was once an altar boy at this church."

I sat there wanting to scream, "His name is Joe and he hates the Catholic Church."

Slim and I sat behind Joe's two sisters with their husbands and kids. At one time, Joe's relatives thought we'd get married; they teased us at his brother's wedding. The morning of the funeral, I hugged Wally, Joe's brother, as we stood in the vestibule. Wally had married his longtime girlfriend—we'd gone to Woodstock with them—but she left him for another man and they divorced. I did not see Tommy at the church but I heard he had dropped by the wake.

Joe had been sick for about a year; people died faster in the early days of the epidemic when the only drug available was AZT. He had never come out to his mother, something I never understood, especially since Joe was encouraging when I came out to my parents. Getting AIDS was a terrible way to break the news. I was thirty-nine when Joe died. I mourned the loss of one of my oldest friends who had helped me find my present path.

"We are now arriving in Penn Station," the conductor announced, shaking me back to the present, where it was hard to believe Joe was dead over twenty years. This reunion with my sorority sisters had triggered an emotionally draining reverie. I felt tired as I exited the train and went upstairs to find a cab.

I often wondered why I did not figure out sooner that I was queer. It must have been the time period, decades before *Ellen* or *The L Word*. I was twenty-five when I came out in 1975, a few years after the Stonewall riots and the birth of the gay rights movement. It was unimaginable that in the year 2010 some states would have same-sex marriage. Nor could I have envisioned gay characters playing leads in sitcoms, and chain bookstores stocking large gay and lesbian sections. We were happy with our women's bookstores and underground filmmakers. Back then, an openly gay male politico was a breakthrough; today, most of my elected city and state officials are gay or lesbian.

A revolution has occurred over the past thirty years. It's a new world, where it's easier to be out. In the '80s and '90s, the age for coming out dropped to fourteen to sixteen years old. Today kids come out at thirteen years old. But that was not the case in the 1970s when researchers say most people came out in their twenties. So actually I was in synch for my generation.

23

RECEIVING INCREDIBLE INFORMATION: NOVEMBER-DECEMBER 2010

I was still on the dating site but I was getting fatigued from slogging through first meetings that went nowhere. But I perked up when Dana e-mailed me; she sounded interesting. Dana was fifty, a light-skinned black woman who lived in Brooklyn and worked as a graphic artist.

When I asked why she contacted me, Dana said she liked my profile because I came across as a hip, cultured Manhattanite. Good answer. She had me at "hip." We set up a date for the next weekend and she suggested the Cornelia Street Café. Fine with me. I liked that place, even though I'd had a drink there with the cyberstalking attorney and the shrink who'd never had a long-term relationship. Hopefully, this date would have more potential.

As I crossed busy Bleecker Street midblock and headed north onto tiny Cornelia Street, I saw a tall, slender black woman walking south toward the café entrance. I strode up to her and asked, "Are you Dana?"

She nodded and we shook hands. "Hi, I'm Kate," I said as we entered.

"Do you want to grab a bite or just have drink?" she asked.

"Food sounds good," I said as we found a table along the window and both ordered beers when the waiter arrived with menus. Dana was about five feet, seven inches, with a pretty face framed by a little Afro flecked with grey. Her only flaw was a crooked tooth.

Dana spoke of her new position at a cable television station. She was happy to be working again after losing her last job when her former company folded. Her new gig designing illustrations for news stories sounded like a creative venture whose main drawback was working until midnight several times a week. I told her how fortunate I felt that I'd landed a full-time teaching job two years ago in the middle of the recession. I almost said that I'd been working the law of attraction to get that position, but I feared she might think I was a New Age nutcase. The waiter came and took our orders. She got a burger and I ordered a spinach salad and the hummus platter.

I told Dana about the homecoming and how I had not seen my sorority sisters in years. Here they were trying to fix me up with the only other lesbian they knew from our school.

"It was hilarious but also very sweet," I said.

"That's nice. They're still your sisters. I went to a women's college too," she said.

"Which one?" I asked.

"Mount Holyoke—on a scholarship."

I'd already deduced she was smart, but going to one of the Seven Sisters impressed me.

"What did you study?" I asked.

"Philosophy and English," she said.

"Two impractical fields," I said. "But then, I majored in English too."

"By the way I'm fifty-seven, not fifty," she said. "I lied on my profile."

Did she want to confess this before I figured out what years we graduated? I hoped it meant she liked me.

The conversation flowed as we discussed our early lives: she grew up in Manhattan with a single mother and two brothers; her mother died when she was in high school and her grandparents became guardians. "It was really hard. We loved Mommy," she said.

"It sounds rough, " I said. "That's a big loss and you were young."

"What about you?"

"Well, on the surface, my early life resembled that show *Father Knows Best*. Except my father was super religious and my mother was a control freak."

Our food arrived and I had trouble watching Dana eat a rare burger. It was pink and uncooked. As a vegetarian for thirty years, I seldom have a reaction when others eat meat, but I had to avert my gaze from her plate. The redness of her burger grossed me out, but I didn't say anything because I liked her.

After we finished dinner, we ordered two more beers and talked about our siblings and their kids—our nieces and nephews. We segued into siblings as a topic when we discussed our upcoming Thanksgiving plans.

Dana sounded close to her brothers, who lived in the city. Her sisters-in-law were Caucasian and Asian, so her nieces were biracial. Dana liked being the cool aunt.

"When I was in the park with my niece, Cindy, someone asked if I was her nanny."

"Ouch," I said.

"But Cindy immediately replied, 'This is my auntie, my real auntie.'"

"Good for her," I said.

We talked about our current schedules and I told her I was a morning person who did her best creative work then. I also mentioned that I taught an early class. I left my house at 7:00 and walked through beautiful Hudson River Park to Tribeca.

"It's early, even for me, but I'm home by 2:30."

"But you're giving your best hours to the man," she said. "Instead of to your art."

I laughed because I had not heard that expression in years, "Well, I only teach three mornings a week," I said. "I have the others to write or do yoga."

I enjoyed talking to Dana. I felt really present and in the moment. I discussed my current goals and where I was going as opposed to where I'd been. I was open and unguarded. As we neared the end of our dinner and waited for the bill, Dana said, "I'm having fun. Let's have a second date."

That felt good to hear and I readily agreed. "Yes, a second date sounds great. Here's my card with my real e-mail. Do you have one?"

"Have to make up a new one," she said, examining mine closely. "Nice card, but you need heavier stock. Hope you don't mind my saying that."

I'd forgotten she was a graphic designer. "I don't mind the suggestion at all. Do you like the vertical style?"

"Yeah, very cool."

We paid the bill and Dana walked me to Staples on Sixth Avenue, where I needed to buy paper. We hugged goodbye in front of the store.

The next day she sent me a sweet e-mail that our dinner was a balm at the end of her workday. A few days later, Dana e-mailed me that she had gone to my site and read my essays. "You really came out on top, Kate," she wrote.

Our second date was Saturday brunch before she went into work at 2 pm. I suggested we meet in Union Square, "west side in front of Staples, away from the green market." Dana kidded that I had a thing for that store, which was true. I love stationery.

We landed up in Coffee Shop, a huge old-fashioned diner, popular with actors and models who had made this place hip, the spot to be visible at a sidewalk table. To my shock, there was no line and we only waited five minutes for a small cozy booth. We both ordered eggs over easy (bad choice); hers were too soft and mine were too hard. But the service was attentive—coffee kept coming—and we never felt rushed; our conversation flowed as easily as the java.

Dana asked my opinion about her plans for grad school and inquired about my experiences at the New School, where I got my master's in Media Studies.

"It was a good program, but I was there a very long time ago," I said.

Dana was lingering over a piece of toast when she asked me about my writing and my subject matter. "Is Slim a nickname?"

"Yeah. We made up that pen name when I was writing this column back in the '90s. Why do you ask?"

Then suddenly Dana mentioned Slim's real name. That stunned me.

"How did you know?" I asked, almost dropping my fork.

"I went out with her a few years ago. Must have been right after you broke up."

"Oh my god," I said, shocked and thinking Slim did not waste any time. "What's your take? I can't believe you remember her name. I can hardly remember the names of people I dated just months ago."

"Let me just say, Kate," and Dana paused dramatically. "I am so glad you are not with her. Even when we met, I thought that this woman she broke up with was lucky to be out from under her spell."

"What?" I was chilled when she used the word "spell." "Tell me more."

"Oh, yeah. She freaked me out," said Dana. "She was so obviously a control freak and she was definitely into me, and she was trying to work her mojo, trying to pull me into her force field, like a magnet."

"Wow," I said. "I can't believe you used those words because when Slim announced she wanted to breakup with me, I felt like she put up this barrier that was pushing me away. It was palpable and I could not get through. It scared me."

"Well, I felt the force field the other way, like she was trying to pull me in," said Dana. "I was so spooked. I even took down my online profile for a while."

"Wow," I replied. "I was so freaked out by Slim's behavior that it sent me back to church. I felt like she was possessed by an outside force."

"I got sucked into her vortex," Dana said. "I could feel she is totally controlling."

"That's for sure, "I said. "I was caught up, always bending over to please her."

"Kate, honey," said my date, as she reached out and touched my arm. "I am so glad to be able to tell you that you are so lucky to be free."

I smiled, "My shrink says the same thing." I was dying to hear more about Dana's reaction and she did not disappoint.

"Besides that," Dana continued. "You are so much more attractive." She then got explicit about Slim's looks and her New York accent. "I wouldn't want to hear that in bed."

I didn't recall her accent as being that grating. When we met, I thought she was beautiful. But she was super dominating. "You must be wondering why I was with her," I said.

"I get it," she said. "You were in love. By the way, she didn't say anything bad about you, and she did say that you started her career."

"Well, at least I'm getting credit," I said.

Learning all this made me feel close to Dana, like she knew what I'd gone through. I even felt I was meant to meet her and get this information from this charming woman. As we shared a dessert of pineapple upside-down cake, Dana told me this dish reminded her of her grandmother who used to make it. We had been there a long time talking and left a generous tip when we split. We still had an hour before Dana went into work.

It was an unseasonably warm November afternoon and everyone was outside. I took off my fall coat as we walked through the green market and found a bench in the busy park. Dana was dressed right for sixty degrees, with a blazer and little bandana around her neck. As she sat down, she took off her jacket and pushed up her shirt sleeves.

Before I had a chance to ask about a puzzling detail from her profile, Dana told me that she usually dated white women because "the sisters" gave her a hard time about how she "talked white."

"Like I'm not saying 'yo' all the time," she explained.

I laughed, reminded of how my students talked at the community college.

"I was impressed you used the word laudatory on our first date," said the English teacher in me. "You seldom hear that word. But aren't you being close-minded about black women?" I asked.

"You're probably right," she said. "But that's been my experience."

When the sun went behind a cloud, I draped my coat over my shoulders as Dana told me more about her prior relationship. I was intrigued to hear her last lover was twenty-five years younger. Some gay women over fifty were too age conscious. I was tired of single lesbian boomer friends, like Janey, asking me, "How old was the crowd?" whenever I mentioned attending a mixer or party.

The hour in the park passed quickly as the sun went in and out. When I said goodbye to Dana at the subway entrance, I leaned in to kiss her on the lips but got her cheek. I was disappointed and hoped I'd get another chance on a third date. But even if I didn't, it was good we had met. The universe brought us together for me to get that information about how I was lucky to be out from under Slim's spell and making a new life on my own.

24

A FOURTH DATE:
NOVEMBER-DECEMBER 2010

"This new person has potential," said Dr. R. when I told her about Dana. "Meeting someone you like is exciting and that makes you feel vulnerable. It's easier to go out with people you are not attracted to."

"I'm still afraid to take a risk because I don't want to get hurt again," I said. "But I'm determined that is not going to stop me."

"Dana seems smart and attractive and it was generous to tell you that about Slim. And she's an artist—what more do you want?" asked my therapist. "You're looking for roadblocks."

Earlier in that session, I'd confessed to Dr. R. that I was relieved when I did not hear back from Dana right away after our second date. My therapist pushed me to admit I was disappointed about the kiss on the cheek. By the time we had our session, Dana and I had planned a third date; I was anxious.

"Don't blow this by finding fault," said Dr. R.

"I hear you," I said.

"You have to learn how to be close while you are independent," she continued. "You don't have much experience in that because you were too embroiled with Slim."

"You're right," I agreed. "That's something I need to work on."

"Take this slowly," Dr. R. said. "A third date is a big step. Be open, have fun, and be aware you feel vulnerable. Don't let fear convince you that you are not interested."

LOOKING FOR A KISS

I dressed carefully for our third meeting, rejecting two shirts and settling for a crisp striped number and tight jeans. Since Dana was an artist, I knew she'd enjoy Canconstruction at the World Financial Center. This annual art show and benefit took place every year before Thanksgiving. Architecture and design companies erected amazing structures using thousands of aluminum cans, which were donated to food pantries when the exhibit came down. Dana had never seen Canconstruction and we agreed to meet at the Winter Garden.

I was sitting under the palm trees at the foot of the grand staircase, our arranged meeting spot, when she texted me that she was there. I stood and turned to my right and saw her waving. I walked over and we kissed hello on the cheek. Then we headed up the escalator to check out the various installations that bordered the upper level around the palm court.

"This so clever," Dana said as we looked at a three-dimensional work made from various colored cans that recreated a pop-up book with "the little engine that could" coming out of the pages. "It's even sharper through the camera. Come, look."

I leaned over her shoulder, peering through her lens and suddenly all the angles of the train became clear. I liked how our bodies touched when I looked through the camera as she held it. We continued strolling through the show with her snapping pictures. We saw models of Russian dolls, children's alphabet blocks, a delivery truck. The most political work depicted the BP oil spill using cans of black beans as the oil.

"Oh my God, this is so cool," I said pointing to a display dubbed the "Candard Hotel." It was a recreation of the Standard Hotel with the High Line Park running underneath it.

"Thanks for turning me on to this show," said Dana as we finished exploring. I was having a good time and was glad when she asked, "Want to get something to eat?"

We left the building and I suggested Kitchenette, a fun place on Chambers Street with good food and vintage decor. As we walked a few blocks north into Tribeca, I kept thinking she was cute and wondered what she thought about me. The restaurant was busy when we arrived but we got a table that had just been vacated.

I ordered mac and cheese and she got a burger deluxe again. While we waited for our food, Dana started telling me about a date she had the day before and how she thought this woman's profile was inaccurate. "She had all this stuff about loving to travel to Europe and it turns out she hasn't been there in twenty years."

As Dana spoke, I wondered why she was sharing this, even though I assumed she was still meeting other people; after all, I was too. Then she said, "I really like you, Kate. I'm glad we met, but I'm not sure if I can keep doing this dating stuff. I'm tired."

I was confused and didn't know if she meant in general or just me. And then Dana asked if I'd be interested in going to holiday parties in Brooklyn filled with people from the publishing industry and the music business. She was appealing to both my interests.

"Sure, why not?" I said. I had no idea if she was asking me as date or a friend. I figured if it was just friendship, I could network with editors. I wanted to attend as her date but her invitation felt vague. "As long as I can get car service back to the city," I added, not making assumptions and wanting to ensure a safe return if I wasn't staying the night with her. As soon as I said it, I regretted that line, thinking it might be interpreted as lack of interest. But I was a cautious person who needed an exit strategy before venturing anywhere new.

Our food arrived and Dana asked if it bothered me to see her eat meat.

"Only the fact that your burger is so rare it looks raw. That grosses me out," I said, feeling good I could be so honest with her.

"Maybe I can hide it behind my hand," she said jokingly.

"I've got a plan," I said and started arranging our soda cans in a row to block her plate from my view. "Look at this—my can construction—it's called the Burger Barrier."

We both dissolved into laughter. I asked if I could taste her garlic fries and offered her a bite of my dish made with four different cheeses. I liked being with her.

But I had no idea where this was going as we walked to the subway station on the corner and swiped our way in. Dana leaned in to hug me goodbye. All I knew was that she was going downtown and I was going uptown.

"Ask her," urged my friend Jessica, when I told her about my confusion. So I did. I realized that by using e-mail to have this important conversation, I was being guarded.

LOOKING FOR A KISS

So I drafted a short e-mail asking what she meant about being tired of dating. Dana wrote back that her tired remark was about continuing to meet new people online—not me—and she hoped we went out some more. That was good to hear. I responded by agreeing with her that all these first dates that go nowhere are draining. I realized then that all our date planning was by e-mail, not phone, which seemed detached. Or maybe it just was easier this way because she worked such crazy shifts.

Dana emailed me after Thanksgiving and asked about another date. I mentioned this show at the Metropolitan Museum and waited to hear back. Meanwhile, I cancelled my online dating site subscription. I was burned out after six months and numerous first dates; plus, I'd finally met someone interesting. Dana said she'd love to get together at the museum where we could enjoy the Friday night chamber music and have a drink. I was thrilled our next date would take place in a classy, romantic setting, not a local downtown eatery.

I got to the Met first and waited for Dana in the vast lobby. I was sitting on a bench near the entrance feeling a bit anxious when she spotted me and came over and gave me a kiss on the cheek. She'd just come from work so we decided to relax first with a glass of wine. Dana knew her way around and led us to the Greek section where on Friday nights the museum converted a balcony into a chamber music café. The hostess seated us near the classical quartet who were setting up their stands.

"I want to be able to see you," Dana said as she sat in the chair across from me.

We both ordered wine and appetizers as the waitress lit the candle on our table.

"This is lovely," I said, looking at the vaulted ceilings and feeling like I was in Europe. As the musicians started to play and the piano and violins resounded through our section, I felt transported in this romantic scene.

"So how was your week?" Dana asked.

"Busy," I said. "I'll be glad when this semester ends. I need a break."

"I could never do your job," she said.

The waitress delivered our drinks and snacks. As we sipped good wine and noshed on spring rolls and samosas, Dana admitted that December was a hard month for her because the anniversary of her mother's death was coming up on December 19th.

"December 19th?" I said, startled. "That's my mother's birthday. How bizarre."

What were the odds that out of 365 days, her mother had died on my mother's birthday? This made me feel more connected, and a bit freaked out. We stopped talking and listened as the pianist pounded out a riveting solo. Everyone applauded when he finished, even the other three musicians.

"Who was that composer?" I asked, knowing Dana played violin.

"Beethoven," she replied. "Shall we get another glass of wine?"

I agreed and she signaled the waitress. I liked that Dana was cultured and could identify classical pieces. I was an expert in '60s and '70s rock and soul music and could recall obscure groups with one hit song—a talent good for game show contestants, not dating.

As we sipped our second glass, I was feeling bold and ready to implement my shrink's suggestion. Dr. R. said that when we were at the Met, I should reach across the table, put my hand over hers and say, "I really like you." My therapist guessed that gesture would get Dana to open up about how she felt scared and vulnerable. When I asked where she got these ideas, she told me she watched a lot of old movies starring Cary Grant. I was scared of rejection, but I grabbed at this idea since it was a plan of action.

One, two, three, I thought to myself as I mustered my courage, leaned across the table put my hand over hers, and said with a smile, "I really like you, Dana."

"I know," she said and that was it. No discussion, no nothing. I felt foolish as I withdrew my hand. I was hurt when Dana responded so insensitively, but I still felt brave for making the overture. But what was going on? I thought I was on the verge of connecting with someone after all those bad dates, but then Dana brushed me off.

We finished our wine and split the bill, which came to $90 with tip and tax. Of course, we were paying for the atmosphere, but dating was expensive. My recent experiences with same-sex dating was that two women split the bill, unless noted otherwise beforehand.

We left the café and asked a guard for directions to the show Dana wanted to see. She kept touching my arm as we walked through the exhibit. I sensed chemistry—or was it the wine? I was turned on but confused because her body language contradicted the dismissive way she had responded to my overture in the café.

We landed up in the modern section, which was sprawling and empty. "This is much better than MOMA," I said, as we sat on a bench and stared at a huge Jackson Pollack. "That place is always packed."

LOOKING FOR A KISS

My mind was reeling when the guard came over and told us we had half an hour left. It was nearing closing time and we never got to the photo exhibit I wanted to see. I hoped we could come back together. I wanted to take things further with her.

Outside the museum, as we walked to the subway, Dana told me that she had mentioned me, her new "dating friend" to her brother. That made me feel important and I hoped it was a good sign. She said he was surprised that she was seeing someone her age, then she added, "I want to date someone who remembers the '80s."

But why refer to me as her "dating friend"? What an ambiguous phrase! She said that she had more dates with me than anyone else. I said, "Same here."

Then Dana said, "Sometimes I'm glad I don't have a girlfriend because I like my solitude." I took that statement as a bad sign. What was with all the mixed signals?

As we parted at the 14th Street subway station, she kissed me on the cheek, gave me a hug, and told me she wanted to see me again although she would be busy around the holidays. Four dates and no real kiss. I was disappointed but not crushed.

So I said, very directly, "I want to move this forward."

"I know, but I'm not in the same place as you."

What did that mean? I felt like she was being evasive, so I asked her point-blank, "Are you ambivalent?"

"I'm open," she said.

Open to what, I wondered as I slipped through the gate to the stairs. Later I thought I should have kissed Dana when she said "I'm open," but I wasn't bold or spontaneous with someone new. I'd already felt rejected once that night. Twice would have been too much.

The next day I e-mailed a date report to my shrink. "You have real guts," she wrote back. She told me not to confront Dana anymore or she'd feel crowded and run away. Then I consulted another voice from my Greek chorus of advisors.

My best friend, Jessica, thought Dana gave too many open-ended answers, and I should know more about what she wanted after four dates. Jessica warned me not to count on it developing. While that was still a possibility, Dana was on a slower time-table than I. Jessica thought it was freaky her mother died on my mother's birthday. "Sounds like you two have some sort of karmic connection." she said. "Plus the fact she had that memorable date with Slim. Too many coincidences."

Two days after the date, I e-mailed Dana that I had had a good time and looked forward to seeing her again. I waited to hear back—but nothing. That felt rude and discouraging.

Two weeks after our date at the museum Dana responded, "If I had gotten back to you sooner, we probably would have gotten together already."

But you didn't, I thought, and why not? It would have been less irritating if she'd told me she was busy at work, but she made a point of saying that things had been slow. She did mention wanting to get together again but did not suggest anything specific.

I should have waited before replying but I was sick of her being evasive. I accused her of sending out conflicting messages by using the term "dating friend." I told her that she came across as elusive, and I thought I was more direct. I was looking for a girlfriend, but she seemed uncertain about what she wanted or uncertain about me. If she still wanted to get together and talk, fine. If not, that was okay too. I hit "Send."

When I reread my message, I thought my tone was angry and I might have burned a bridge. I sounded too pissed off and was considering calling Dana and talking in person. I needed to be less upset when things did not go my way with people I barely knew.

To my dismay, Dana replied back that she didn't think I was sending out "girlfriend energy" when I asked about transportation back to Manhattan if I went to a Brooklyn party with her. "I'm looking for someone who wants to maybe not make it back home."

Dana indicated that in the interest of directness she did not see herself going further with me, although she admitted she'd been unclear and understood my frustration. I apologized for the harsh tone in my last e-mail and told her I too was open to friendship.

Even though I was disappointed this didn't go further, I was glad I'd met Dana. I had gotten to a record post-breakup fourth date. I was more open and receptive than in the past.

25

IN MY CELLS:
DECEMBER 2010

Kia flung open the door, ushered me in, and greeted me with a big hug. I hopped up on a massage table and lay on my back in a large sunny room with brick walls. Colorful art and statues of saints decorated the space. Kia was working from the ground-floor office of a colleague's Park Slope brownstone, in a place called "Sacred Space for Women."

Kia started the reading by running her hand up and down my body, her palm a few inches above me. I could feel energy flowing from me to her.

"Your first and second chakras are closed and so is your throat chakra," she said.

I was relieved to hear my heart chakra was open since I'd been working on that.

"I know the first chakra is the root and the second has something to do with sex," I said, "but why is my throat closed?"

"The closed lower ones affect your throat chakra," she explained. That made sense since chakras are astral nerve centers, similar to a phone line with connected wires.

"You have a jittery stomach," she added (which was true). "The stomach is the bridge between the upper and lower. Calming this down will help manifestation by getting the energy to flow and not break apart. Try some simple cleanses, like wheatgrass juice."

Ugh. I hated wheatgrass juice, but I'd do whatever was necessary.

Kia saw a parallel between my two goals—finishing my book and meeting someone. She saw me carrying the pages of the book in a dark tote bag with a latch.

(Her description fit my navy blue messenger bag that I used to bring the pages to the copy shop.)

As we continued talking about finding a new relationship, Kia said, "This person is going to approach you and it feels organic. I don't think you will meet her online."

That was good to hear since I was burned out from computer dating.

"Any places where I should put myself to run into her?" I asked.

"Just keep a positive focus and follow your leads," Kia said, as she kept walking around the massage table and waving her hand in circles above my body. She kept closing her eyes, as if picturing something, and then opening them again.

"There is a more polished side of you," she said. "Energetically, you've done a lot of shedding since I saw you last summer. Your past relationship pounded you down. I'm hearing the word 'bamboozled,'" continued Kia. "I never use that word but it popped into my head. Does that mean anything to you?"

"Yes, it does. I felt bamboozled by my ex, especially the way she ended things."

"You are still carrying something slight from her, a little stab, but it's almost gone. Now you are in a real receptive mode. Your mind and body are more into being in a relationship than before. It's not just your mind talking—it's in your cells now."

"In my cells. Wow. I'm so glad to hear this," I said. "I was afraid that I was not doing enough spiritual work once I went back to my teaching job."

"You did a lot of good work," she repeated, closing her eyes again and taking a deep breath. "Oh, wow! I'm getting a vision of you at a commitment ceremony."

"Really?" I said, hoping her image would come true.

"Everything is lining up for you in the next year, " she said.

"That's great," I said as I told Kia how I'd been listening to this new law of attraction CD from Esther and Jerry Hicks called *Getting into the Vortex*. "The idea is that if you are affirming from inside the vortex, whatever you are trying to attract will show up—it's like a short cut."

"Cool," said Kia. "How do you get there?"

"When you listen to the CD and pay attention to your breath, you release resistance and that raises your vibrations," I explained. "The basic concept is to elevate your personal vibration to be in alignment with the frequency of your inner source."

"And then you are in the vortex?" asked Kia.

"Exactly," I said. "I feel this is the key to my unlocking the law of attraction in this area, to blasting past any lingering resistance about meeting someone."

As I said that, I realized what my shrink called baddar, the guides called resistance. It was the same idea from different approaches, psychological and spiritual.

"That sounds very useful," said Kia. "I can't wait to listen to it."

We ended with Kia blessing me with scented oils and my wishing her a safe trip back to her native Hawaii. "I'll see you again at Omega next summer," I said.

"You'll be with someone," she winked.

I left the session thinking that every reader I had seen said the same thing about my meeting someone. I also knew the timeline was the most unreliable part. I did not dismiss this as "happy talk" but rather as everyone being on the same page.

Of course, as a college professor who taught Critical Thinking, I tried to balance faith and reason and knew my trust in psychics, astrologers, card readers, and healers required an approach where my faith transcended reason. I also realized those I consulted were only human beings with highly developed intuition in specific areas. But their insights gave hope.

Thousands of devout people who would never consult psychics believed in miracles: God parted the Red Sea for the Israelites and Jesus turned water into wine at a wedding. While the readers I saw made no claims to be divine, I thought them inspired and the concept was similar—it required a leap of faith.

◊◊♦♦

On a cold December morning, I left Integral Yoga after an invigorating class. I crossed West 13th Street and headed to the gay center to pick up the new issue of *GO* Magazine, the popular dyke city monthly.

"Excuse me," said a woman who was sitting in a parked car, door open, about two hundred feet from the entrance.

The car was too far from the curb, so I thought she wanted help parking or she was seeking directions. I walked toward her. She was about forty, with shoulder-length dirty blonde hair that needed washing. Her car was filled with blankets like she'd been sleeping in it.

"Are you gay?" she asked out of nowhere.

"Yeah. Why?" I said, surprised at her question.

"Do you have a girlfriend?" she asked.

"I'm dating someone," I lied, wondering where this was going. This woman seemed highly agitated as she gripped the phone in her hand.

"But you see other people?" she asked.

"What's this all about?" I demanded.

"I'm confused," she said. "I want to figure out if I'm gay. I want a woman to kiss me and then I'll know. Would you kiss me? I'm going crazy. I have to know."

I was taken aback by her request. "You should talk to a therapist. They could help you at the Institute for Human Identity. They specialize in these issues."

"No, no therapy," she said. "I want a kiss. I want a woman to hold me. "

I shook my head and adjusted my yoga mat which was slipping off my shoulder. "You can't just expect strange people to kiss you—"

I was stunned at this ironic interaction. I'd been looking for love and romance all year and now this unhinged woman was throwing herself at me. Was the universe mocking my efforts? Was the devil tempting me, like Eve with the apple? For a brief moment I considered it, if only to end this drought, yet then I realized no good could come from kissing a crazy lady in the street. What if she had a knife or gun hidden in her car? That thought made me back away from the vehicle.

"Well, if you won't do it, maybe you know someone who will. I could give you my card—please? I have to know."

"This isn't the right way to go about this," I said thinking she'd have better luck making her appeal at the Cubbyhole on the night they served cheap shots of tequila.

She was sitting on the edge of her car seat facing me, her feet on the curb, her head in her hands.

"For two years I have been trying to figure this out," she said sounding desperate. "First I was into Jesus and then I was married and—"

When she mentioned Jesus, I thought what would he do in this situation? I was not sure if he'd touch her, but I knew Jesus would act with kindness and compassion.

"You gotta do things to meet women," I said. "Go to a dance or a bar or an event at the center." By now, we'd been talking about five minutes. "Look, I have to go. I'm freezing, shivering. Good luck and please talk to a therapist."

"No, I want a kiss and then I will know. Please. I'm clean. I don't have diseases. We could go somewhere. I'm not a hooker."

"No, sorry," I said. "I can't." I hadn't had a soulful kiss in a long time, yet I wasn't so desperate that I'd make out with a deranged woman stalking lesbians outside the gay center. I turned and walked inside the building, grateful to be safe inside the warm lobby.

I went up to the handsome Latino man behind the front desk and spoke to him. "I'm sure you see and hear a lot of weird shit in your position, but something pretty strange just happened to me outside—" and I told him the story of the woman who wanted a kiss to determine if she was a lesbian.

"Oh, her?" he said, obviously familiar. "She's back? She's been doing that off and on for years. People have been nice to her, like you. I'm amazed no one has hit her. She's more than confused. She's crazy. I feel bad for her."

"Yeah, she looks tortured," I said, feeling sorry for her too. When I slipped back outside, ten minutes later, I was relieved to see her car was gone.

As I relived this weird encounter over the next few winter evenings, I convinced myself that she was a messenger—a crazy queer Christmas angel—sent to make love clearer for me. She was desperate for a kiss but I wasn't. I was fine on my own, just being me.

ABOUT THE AUTHOR

Kate Walter has been living in downtown Manhattan since 1975 when she escaped across the river from New Jersey. *Looking for a Kiss* is her debut memoir.

Walter's essays and opinion pieces have appeared in *The New York Times*, *Newsday*, *New York Daily News*, *AM-NY*, the *Advocate*, and many other outlets. She teaches writing at CUNY and NYU.

DISCLAIMER

Names and identifying characteristics of some people in this book have been changed to protect privacy. A few events have been reordered or collapsed for literary cohesion.

ACKNOWLEDGMENTS

Major thanks to Naomi Rosenblatt, a fantastic publisher, who got my book immediately and was a pleasure to work with. Eternal gratitude to Susan Shapiro, my friend, colleague, and amazing critic who runs the Thursday night workshop where this book was critiqued.

Thank you to all the writers who gave me feed back on this manuscript: Judy Batalion, Hilary Davidson, Alice Feiring, Merideth Finn, Alyson Gerber, Sara Karl, Kristen Kemp, Amy Klein, Lisa Lewis, Erica Manfred, Liza Monroy, Tony Powell, Rich Prior, Abby Sher, Devan Sipher, Royal Young.

Thank you to anyone who read pages whose name I may have omitted. This has been a long writing journey of many years and several drafts.

Thank you to my editors: Lincoln Anderson at *The Villager* and Jerry Portwood formerly at *NY Press* who published parts of this book in essay form. That steady support inspired me in the early stages and helped shape this memoir.

Thank you to Julie Dubow for computer assistance at all hours.

Thank you to my spiritual teachers, my yoga teachers, and my incredible therapist, Dr. Ronnie C. Lesser.

Thank you to my friends and family for always being there, especially my mother, Agnes Walter, for being a role model of resilience.

www.ingramcontent.com/pod-product-compliance
Lightning Source LLC
Chambersburg PA
CBHW071704090426
42738CB00009B/1652